CW00544244

Royal Deeside Railway

Aberdeen to Ballater

Summer days on Deeside. The battery-electric rail-car basks in the dock platform at Ballater whilst awaiting its turn back to Aberdeen on the 5.35pm. July 15th, 1959. (The late Roy Hamilton)

Contents

Great North of Scotland Railway.

LUGGAGE.

CRATHES

FROM ABERDEEN.

Introduction

THE DEE, one of the country's best known rivers, rises in the Wells of Dee at around 4000 feet amid the wild and beautiful Cairngorm landscape between Braeriach and Cairn Toul. From there it tumbles down into the Lairig Ghru, a great pass through the mountains, but it is not until it reaches the Linn of Dee some dozen miles down stream that it becomes accessible to any other than hill walkers. It is here that Deeside as known by the tourist begins.

Below the Linn the valley is comparatively narrow. The river runs through woods and forests of birch and pine with Lochnagar and the mountains around An Sochach to the south while to the north Beinn A'Bhuird and Ben Avon dominate the skyline. Around Ballater the mountains recede and lower. The character of the river changes — no longer shallow and fast flowing it becomes wider and more sedate. Agriculture begins to take over from forestry, although woods are never absent. Add to all this the presence of some of the finest salmon fishing and the combination led to the saying that if any river flows through paradise it must be the Dee.

No wonder Queen Victoria chose Balmoral as her holiday residence giving the valley its sobriquet — 'Royal Deeside'.

Inevitably the valley's commerce attracted the railway promoters and in 1853 the Deeside Railway opened as far as Banchory with the trains reaching Ballater 13 years later. With the railway came the visitors in ever increasing numbers, no doubt encouraged by advertisements such as this one published in 1866:

> The scenery's grand, the air, oh! it's charming,
> Deeside being famed for excellent farming;
> The mountains stupendous, and sweet heathery plains —
> The travelling's pleasant, there's well arranged trains.

Sadly, one hundred years later this ceased to be the case.

The journey from Aberdeen to Ballater may not have had the grandeur found on the West Highland Line or the one to Kyle of Lochalsh but it was none the poorer for that. The train allowed visitors to savour Deeside's pleasures in a way that is not possible driving a car along today's busy main road. Hopefully, therefore, this booklet will give them something of the story and character of a railway journey which can no longer be enjoyed.

Dick Jackson

Front cover: **BR standard 2-6-4 tank engine No. 80029 stands at Dinnet with an up train.** *(The late Peter McIntyre. Courtesy Mrs McIntyre)*

Back cover: **Balmoral Castle as painted by Kenneth Steel on a BR poster.** *(Keith Jones Collection)*

Travel before the railway

The Dee valley has been a trade route linking the north-east highlands with the coast at Aberdeen for generations but, before the arrival of the railway, transport was difficult; those who had to travel having the option of walking or riding on horseback. Goods went either on lumbering wagons or, if more easily transportable, loaded into panniers slung across the back of a horse. By the latter half of the 17th century tracks had developed and there was a well used pack-horse road, parts of which are still in use and little altered apart from some widening and modern surfacing. The most obvious sections are to be found on the minor road linking Bridge of Canny and Kincardine O'Neill and along the Pass of Ballater. There are also the remains of a small bridge in a garden to the west of Crathie Church and another, complete one, near Crathes which could only be seen from the train. This old road was gradually replaced by the turnpike which opened in stages; reaching Crathes by 1798 and Aboyne four years later. There it stopped for about 50 years before being extended to Braemar and south over the Cairnwell Pass.

By 1824 a Mr James Irvine is recorded as running a coach from Aberdeen to Kincardine O'Neill on three mornings each week. The journey of 23 miles took five hours and cost 10/6 inside or 6/6 outside. Twenty five years later the *Prince of Wales* and *The Queen of Beauty* reached Banchory in two hours, the former using the south Deeside road. During the summer the *Marquis of Huntly* left Aboyne at 5am "every lawful day" on its 4 hour journey to Aberdeen. In addition to the coaches, about 30 carriers were by now plying their trade up and down Deeside but neither the old road nor the turnpike solved the problem of getting timber, a major traffic, to its main market in Aberdeen. The solution lay in floating the logs down river, usually from defined floating banks.

The arrival of the railway in 1853 altered all this. Travellers from Aberdeen could now reach Banchory in an hour with corresponding shorter journeys as the line was extended up river, while timber became an important source of income to the Deeside company and its successors.

Rails to Banchory

By 1845 thoughts were turning to building a railway up Deeside and in September of that year a group of Aberdeen businessmen met to consider the possibilities, and a provisional committee was set up under the chairmanship of Lord Provost Blaikie, who was also chairman of the Great North of Scotland Railway. They were satisfied that it would be a viable proposition and issued a prospectus for the **Deeside Railway** giving their estimate of costs, traffic and financial outlook for a railway linking Aberdeen and Banchory. The original capital of £100,000, issued in shares of £50 each, was so popular that the whole amount had been raised within a week, no doubt aided by the expected return of 9%. So great was the interest that the *Aberdeen Herald* commented "…there is only wanting the means of cheap and speedy conveyance to cause the whole of Deeside to be studded with villas and cottages as thickly as the Banks of Clyde…. God speed the Deeside Railway". In fact so well did the public subscribe that later in the month it was decided the line should be extended to Aboyne with the capital increased to £220,000. Once again the public responded favourably and Parliament having agreed the proposal the Deeside Railway Act received Royal Assent on 16th July 1846.

Sadly these high hopes were to suffer a lengthy delay. First of all the directors decided to postpone work until the Aberdeen Railway was nearer completion so as to be able to make use of the heavy plant being used in its construction, thus reducing costs, but that company had its own monetary problems and in order to speed matters up the Deeside lent it £16,000 which led to a large number of the Deeside shareholders demanding that their company be wound up. The Aberdeen Railway thereupon took up most of the unallocated Deeside shares and so won control. It was about this time Balmoral became royal property, an event which rekindled public interest in the Deeside Railway and led to the Aberdeen company selling its holding. Fresh directors under the chairmanship of John Duncan, a well known Aberdeen advocate, were then elected.

The new board decided to terminate the line at Banchory and this, along with other details, required a fresh Deeside Railway Act which was approved in May 1852, seven years after the optimistic start to the whole idea. In the end the first turf was cut on 5th July 1852 in a field near Mains of Drum. There were few construction problems and trains began running on 8th September 1853 reaching Banchory in an hour — a vast improvement on the old coaches. Originally the Deeside trains used the Aberdeen Company's terminus at Ferryhill but in 1854 both Companies moved to a new station at Guild Street, nearer the city centre and more or less on the site of the former goods yard.

Mrs Kinloch has just cut the first turf of the Deeside Railway. Mains of Drum, 5th July 1852.

Four months before opening a search began for suitable engines and two were ordered from Hawthorn of Leith. These could not be delivered in time and so an arrangement was made with the Scottish Central Railway to work the trains with engines and rolling stock provided by itself and also the Aberdeen and Scottish Midland Railways (these two amalgamated in 1856 to form the Scottish

From 1854 until the Joint station was opened thirteen years later, Deeside trains used the Scottish North Eastern Railway's Guild Street station. The ship masts show its proximity to the docks. Note the oil pot lamp fittings and the ribs on the roofs of these early carriages.

North Eastern Railway which, along with the Scottish Central, became part of the Caledonian Railway some ten years later).

There were problems with this arrangement from the start and only seven weeks after the opening the shareholders were told that the Company would work its own traffic and two engines had been ordered. When the SCR submitted its first account in November for work done there was indeed trouble. Not only was it based on a quite different basis from that agreed but was for greater mileage than that actually worked! There was much wrangling over the ensuing months until at the beginning of March 1854 the Scottish Central refused to carry on. Luckily the first of the Hawthorns had by then been delivered.

DEESIDE RAILWAY.

_____ *Station,* _____ 185 .

RETURN TICKET.

and Party of _____

From _____

To _____

THIRD CLASS.

No. _____

On to Aboyne and Ballater

By 1856 it was clear that support was forthcoming for taking the line on from Banchory to Aboyne and for this purpose the nominally independent **Deeside Extension Railway** was formed, the necessary Act being passed in the following year. Under the original proposals of 1845 it had been intended to follow the river through Kincardine O'Neill which would have necessitated two crossings of the Dee. In order to reduce costs, the line was re-routed via Torphins which not only avoided the bridges but the land was cheaper to buy. Against that, trains faced some stiff gradients, especially on either side of the summit near Lumphanan. Work started in October 1857 and following the normal Board of Trade inspection the line was opened on 2nd December 1859, although Captain Tyler had some reservations about the state of the track.

The relationship between the two Companies was rather unusual. The new Company was in fact part of the Deeside which subscribed to the Extension, built it and worked it at cost. Although most of the directors sat on both Boards there were different groups of shareholders and the finances of both Companies were kept separate even to the extent of keeping apart their traffics at Banchory. Dividends were paid only on the profits for the section concerned and since the Deeside Railway was always a profitable concern with dividends up to $7\frac{1}{2}$ per cent compared to the shares in the Extension which never reached 3 per cent, this showed the wisdom of the arrangement for the former's shareholders.

Five years after opening to Aboyne yet another Company, the **Aboyne and Braemar Railway** was set up to complete the route and take the railway through Upper Deeside to the village of Braemar. However, during discussion on the Bill it was decided to go no further than Bridge of Gairn, a mile or so beyond Ballater. This short length would be for goods traffic only, with any further extension up the valley needing special legislation. This was never made and the full story is related later under the heading 'Unfulfilled Dreams'.

It seems that the line was "built on the cheap" as when Captain Tyler inspected it in September 1866 he did not like what he found. In particular more work was called for on some of the bridges and also parts of the track to bring them up to standard, while much of the fencing needed to be improved. All this was quickly taken care of and trains finally reached Ballater on 17th October. It was an inauspicious start. At the next half-yearly meeting shareholders were told that not only was it the worst period of the year for traffic but that the line had been completely blocked by snow for at least half of January. Furthermore the anticipated timber traffic had not materialised. All this meant that for the first quarter the Revenue Account balance amounted to only £118:4:6.

Changes in ownership

Meanwhile events had been taking place which eventually led to a change in ownership of the Deeside Railway. The Great North in its earlier years was a very cantankerous concern, unwilling to co-operate with its neighbours and even, so its detractors said, its passengers! Its Aberdeen terminus was on the dockside at Waterloo, several hundred yards along the quay from the Scottish North Eastern and Deeside station at Guild Street to which it was connected by a horse-drawn tramway. The SNER wanted to improve connections across the city but was baulked by the GNSR which would not co-operate, so in 1862 it secured Parliamentary approval for a new railway from Stonehaven to near Kintore, on the GNSR's main line to Keith, thus by-passing Aberdeen. This would have crossed the Deeside near Culter and if the SNER could secure running powers from there into Aberdeen it would have nicely solved the problem — apparently a straightforward arrangement but the financial terms offered were not acceptable to the Deeside company.

At this juncture railway politics came into it. John Duncan, the Deeside chairman, apparently on his own initiative, approached the Great North with an offer to lease his line thus hoping for better terms from the SNER. The latter's threat to the GNSR was so serious that his proposal was accepted even though the Deeside board was not exactly enthusiastic. Although it was obvious that it would be sensible to make the arrangement permanent, because of the attitude of the Deeside directors, and of course the SNER, this was not at first possible. Terms were finally agreed in 1866 and the GNSR leased the Deeside for 999 years as from 1st September of that year.

Meantime the Deeside Railway had undertaken to work the Aboyne and Braemar Railway which opened for traffic on 16th October 1866, six weeks after the lease came into force. Thus it was the Great North which worked the Ballater trains from the start.

The GNSR later amalgamated with all three companies; taking over the Deeside and the Extension as from 31st August 1875, followed by the Aboyne and Braemar on 31st January 1876. The Great North itself ceased

John Duncan, first chairman and 'father' of the Deeside Railway and later, Chairman of the GNSR.

to exist on 1st January 1923, becoming the Northern Scottish Area of the newly formed London and North Eastern Railway while that company, in turn, was swallowed up by British Railways on 1st January 1947.

*In 1920 Mr Walker was the station master at Cults. A train must be
expected since there are several passengers on the platform as well as
members of his staff.*

Along the line

Deeside trains began their journey at the Joint Station and followed the
main line to the south for the first $^3/_4$ mile to Ferryhill Junction where they
turned sharply west into the Dee valley, and for the next 7 miles to Culter ran
through the pleasant southern suburbs of Aberdeen, often with gardens coming down to the lineside, and all the time with views across the river. After
passing three suburban stations they reached **Cults** where passengers could
see the "Shakkin' Briggie", a small suspension bridge built across the river
in 1837 to allow those living in the village to attend the parish church which
at that time was situated on the other side of the Dee. It was funded by the
minister, Dr Morrison, who had been left a substantial legacy which he spent
for the benefit of the community.

Four more suburban stations followed, one of which, **Milltimber**, had its
usefulness increased in 1895 by the construction of Maryculter bridge over the
Dee. This was one of four crossings built, at least in part, to allow residents
on the south bank of the river to use the trains.

Culter was always busy, especially while it was the terminus of the suburban
trains, fondly known as the "Subbies". Their arrival in 1894 led to the present
station being built a short distance to the east of the original. It also handled
the not inconsiderable traffic generated by the local paper-mill.

From here on to Banchory the line went through open country, never very
far from the road or river, and soon came to **Drum** which served a scattered

A 'Subby' passes another train at Milltimber.

Period piece at Culter in 1908. Mails, milk, and a passenger await the next train.

Drum Station, Deeside.

A postcard shows a down train stopping at Drum in GNS days.

rural community. In its earlier days it was well used, issuing over 6,600 tickets in 1864 for example. With the arrival of cars and buses the local people found these more convenient and numbers fell off until by 1938 less than 400 were sold, producing an income of around £17. No wonder it was completely closed as early as 1951.

The road connecting **Park** station with the South Deeside Road was built by the railway company with the prime purpose of allowing residents on the south side of the river to use the trains. After crossing the Dee on an attractive bridge with two graceful cast-iron arches, the road, as motorists will notice, is

Park is typical of the neat style of building found along Deeside. At one time it was the end of the double track from Ferryhill but when seen here in 1965 the second line was a crossing loop.

Banchory station during its reconstruction in 1902/1903.

Torphins boasted two footbridges, the further one serving as part of a right-of-way. The characteristic GNSR wooden construction can be contrasted with the later LNER replacements made from old rails, seen on the picture of Lumphanan (page 15).

built like a railway with embankments and cuttings instead of following the ground surface! As the road and bridge were private property the Company charged a toll which continued to be collected by British Railways until some time in the 1950s when the cost per car was 3d. (1.2p). Both the bridge and adjoining toll house are now Listed Buildings.

Crathes was originally a private halt for the Laird of Crathes but became a public station in 1863 when the nearby **Mills of Drum** was closed. Here again the station was connected with the far bank of the river by a bridge erected especially to allow easy access to the trains. The original Durris bridge was built in 1862 and funded by Alexander Mactier, who owned the estate on the south bank. He levied a toll for its use so that those of his tenants who crossed at Park bridge "would not be disadvantaged". At least that is what he said!

About 300 yards beyond the station the line crossed a small burn and immediately downstream of the railway there still exists an interesting relic of the Old Deeside Road in the form of a small stone packhorse bridge — the only complete one remaining along the length of the road. Built in the later years of the 17th century it was in use until the turnpike opened in 1802.

Banchory was a large station as befitted the flourishing town it served, although it was sited rather awkwardly. It was re-built in 1902/03, a short distance west of the original and was unusual in being lit by acetylene gas up until it closed. This was made in a little building alongside the track and led to the station's 'trade mark' — a small heap of white, spent carbide. Half a mile further on BR opened a diminutive halt at **Dee Street** in 1961. Although devoid of any form of shelter and with a platform not even long enough to take a 2-car diesel set it was in a more convenient location for much of the town. As events turned out it had a very brief life, closing five years later.

The trains now turned away from the river and for the next $2\frac{1}{2}$ miles were faced with a stiff climb through woods and rough country before reaching **Glassel**, another quiet station serving a scattered population. For a few years prior to 1887 there was a private platform at Craigmyle, about 2 miles further on, for the benefit of the occupants of Craigmyle House.

Before the arrival of the railway, **Torphins** had been little more than a group of houses around a cross-roads. The train service changed all that and it became a fashionable place for members of Aberdeen's business community to build a country home and still be within easy reach of the city.

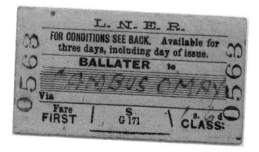

Beltie Viaduct near Torphins on the steep climb to Satan's Den, with Learney Hill in the background.

Further steep climbing followed across the Beltie Burn and on up into the deep cutting known as "Satan's Den". At over 600 feet above sea level it was prone to blockages during winter snows.

Beyond Satan's Den the railway dropped equally steeply down to **Lumphanan**, a village whose chief claim to fame is that nearby in 1057 Macbeth, King of Scots, was killed in single-handed combat by the Earl of Moray — a cairn now marking the spot. On leaving the station the line once again made a sharp change of direction to head south-west past **Dess**, another isolated station, and dropped down towards the Dee, passing Aboyne Loch which, in hard winters, was used for Bonspiels with a special platform provided for use by the curlers and occasional summer excursions.

The fine station at **Aboyne** was re-built in the late 1890s in keeping with the pleasant town it served. On leaving, the trains passed through a short tunnel, one of only four on the GNSR.

A DMU driver's view of 'Satan's Den' cutting east of Lumphanan. No wonder it was a fearsome place in a blizzard, easily filling with snow.

Lumphanan in its later days. The old goods yard, on the right, closed in 1964, while the signals were removed in February 1966 — which dates the photo since complete closure came just over four months later.

A view along the line to the original Aboyne station. Although the facilities were quite simple, the station could boast an overall roof.
(Aberdeen University Library, G.W. Wilson Collection)

Aboyne station was re-built in this handsome style around 1900. Very little had changed by the 1960s when this photograph was taken. The building remains today, in commercial use.

An up train has just passed the 'dockit hoose' as it approaches Cambus O'May. The old quarries are clearly seen on the hillside. (Aberdeen Journals)

Heading on towards **Dinnet** the railway remained close to the road on one side and not far from the river on the other. After crossing a stretch of moorland it once again reached the Dee at **Cambus O'May**, surely one of the most picturesque stations in the country, perched on a narrow shelf right above the water. Its unusual name derives from Gaelic 'Cam a Maigh' meaning 'Bend in the Plain' which accurately describes the double bend in the river with flat ground on either side.

The nearby suspension footbridge over the river was built in 1905 to replace the old ferry. With a view to encouraging visitors to the attractive river banks it was partly funded by the Great North. In recent years it gradually fell into disrepair until in 1988 it was found to be cheaper to replace it with the present span which, unlike the original, does not cross the track bed.

Close by is a house with an interesting history. Originally an Inn, it was separated from the river by the old road. When the turnpike was built it passed behind the building, hard up against a rock face but even so there was insufficient room for the railway when it arrived. The solution lay in cutting off one corner of the house — and so it remains to this day, known locally as the "dockit hoose".

The Culblean hills now crowd in on the north side of the line and show the remains of old quarry workings which produced a fine pinkish-red granite. On the other side fine views of the hills of upper Deeside come into view, dominated by the massive bulk of Lochnagar.

Before long comes the hamlet of Tullich with the ruins of a pre-Reformation church. Tradition has it that on a wild winter Sunday in the absence of the minister, the waiting congregation started to dance to keep themselves warm and to the excited strains of the cobbler's fiddle they improvised the famous Reel of Tullich.

The railway finally reached its terminus at **Ballater,** 43 ¼ miles from Aberdeen. The long curving platform, built to accommodate the royal train, ends at an overbridge, a sad reminder of the "railway that never was" on to

Ballater with a diesel rail-car about to leave for Aberdeen.

Braemar. The original station was a poor affair, quite unfit for royal use so was re-built in the mid-1880s and is now restored.

Outside the buildings, in Station Square, the boundary of railway property is marked by a series of stones set into the road surface. Each has the letters "GNSR" carved into it and in times gone by were the subject of considerable dispute between the citizens and the Great North. Details are scanty but the Company must have won their case since the stones are still there.

Ballater Station staff in 1907.

Train services

When the railway opened to Banchory in 1853 the first timetable showed three return trains every week-day, taking about an hour for the journey of 16 miles and all carrying 1st and 3rd class passengers. (As on the Great North there never was a 2nd class). Five years later the number of trains had increased to five with times ranging between 50 and 95 minutes, the latter being a mixed train conveying goods wagons as well as passengers. Arrangements were made with a Mr Cook of the Huntly Arms Hotel at Aboyne to run connecting coaches which in the down direction left Banchory following the arrival of the 7.45am and 4.15pm trains. The former reached Ballater at "about 12.28pm" while the latter only went as far as Aboyne, reached at 7.30pm. In the reverse direction the Aboyne coach left at 6.45am for the 8.57am to Aberdeen while the Ballater

ABERDEEN TO BANCHORY.

	Trains will not depart from, nor arrive at. the following Stations before the Hours undernoted respectively.	DOWN TRAINS.				
Miles.		1. 1 & 3 Class Mail.	2. 1 and 3 Class.	3. Mixed 1 & 3 Class	4. 1 & 3 Class Mail.	5. 1 & 3 Class
	TRAINS LEAVE	A.M.	A.M.	P.M	P.M.	P.M.
	Aberdeen,	7·45	11· 0	1·45	4 15*	7· 0
	Ruthrieston,	7 52	—	—		7· 7
	Cults,	8· 0	11·15	2· 5	4·29	7·15
	Murtle.	8· 4	11·20	2 12	4·34	7·19
	Milltimber,	—	11·25	2 19	—	7·23
	Culter,	8·11	11·29	2 29	4·40	7 27
	Drum,	—	11·41	2·45	4 52	7·37
	Park,	8·22	11 46	2·50	4 57	7 41
	Mills of Drum,	8·30	11 54	2 55	5· 5	7 50
	Banchory, ...arrive at	8·40	12· 5	3·15	5·15	8 0

Coach Arrives at Potarch about	10· 0	...	...	6·30	...
Do. Kincardine O'Neil,	10·15	...	...	6·50	..
Do. Aboyne, ...	10·46	...	...	7·30	...
Do. Ballater, ...	12 28P M.	..	...	...	...

Coach Leaves Ballater, ...	...	...	8.30	...	...
Do. Aboyne, ...	...	6 45	10· 0	...	...
Do. Banchory, ..arrive	...	8 45	12·10	...	...

BANCHORY TO ABERDEEN.

	Trains will not depart from, nor arrive at. the following Stations before the Hours undernoted respectively.	UP TRAINS				
Miles.		1. Mixed 1 & 3 Class.	2. 1 & 3 Class Mail.	3. 1 and 3 Class. Mail.	4. 1 & 3 Class.	5 1 & 3 Class.
	TRAINS LEAVE	A.M	A.M.	P.M.	P.M.	P.M.
	Banchory.	7·20	8 57	12 30	5 45	8·30
	Mills of Drum,	7·32	9· 6	12·40	—	8 40
	Park,	7·43	9·13	12 48	6· 0	8 48
	Drum.	7·49	9.17	12 53		8 53
	Culter,	8· 0	9·24	1· 3	6 10	9· 5
	Milltimber,	8 18	—	1· 8	—	9· 8
	Murtle.	8·25	9·30	1·12	6 16	9·13
	Cults,	8 32	9·37	1 18	6 23	9·20
	Ruthrieston,	—	—	—		9·27
	Aberdeen, ...arrive at	8·55	9·50	1 30	6·35	9 35

* ☞ ON SATURDAYS, No. 4 Down Train will leave Aberdeen at 4·30 p.m. instead of 4 15 p.m., arriving at all the other Stations 15 minutes later than usual.

Nos. 1. and 3. Up Trains will stop only by Signal at Drum and Milltimber when there are Goods or Passengers to forward or put off No. 1. Up Train will shunt at Culter to allow No. 1. Down Train to pass.

The original railway terminated at Banchory, and this 1858 timetable gives the connecting times of the coach to Ballater.

coach departed at 8.30am to connect with the 12.30pm from Banchory.

Following the opening to Aboyne in 1859 three out of the four trains in each direction ran right through, taking 2 to 2½ hours. By the next summer there were six trains in each direction, two terminating at Banchory while the rest ran through to and from Aboyne. For several years thereafter the service did not exceed five trains each way.

When the railway reached Ballater in 1866 the timetable showed three through trains each way with another terminating at Aboyne and a fourth going only as far as Banchory. The Ballater trains took anything up to 2½ hours giving an average speed of just over 17 mph but even that was much faster than the old coach service.

It was not only Deeside

DEESIDE RAILWAY.

OPENING TO ABOYNE.

ALTERATION OF TRAINS.

ON and after **FRIDAY**, the 2d December, 1859, and until further notice, the Departures and Arrivals of PASSENGER TRAINS will be as follows, viz.:—

	1 Classes 1 & 3 Mail. A.M.	2 Classes 1 & 3 Mixed. A.M.	3 Classes 1 & 3 Mixed. P.M.	4 Classes 1 & 3 Mail. P.M.
Trains Depart				
From ABERDEEN (Guild Street Station)......	7·45	11·0	2·0	4·30
Arrive at BANCHORY...	8·50	12·15	3·30	5·32
Arrive at ABOYNE	9·45	1·22	...	6·42
Per Coach.				
Ballater............	11·45	...	...	...

. Seats per Coach to places beyond Aboyne may be secured at the Booking Office, Aberdeen.

Leaves				
Per Coach ⎰ Ballater............	...	...	9·0	...
Cambus O'May ...	...	...	9·35	...
⎱ Dinnet	...	...	10·10	...

	1 Classes 1 & 3 Mixed. A.M.	2 Classes 1 & 3 Mail. A.M.	3 Classes 1 & 3 Mail. P.M.	4 Classes 1 & 3 P.M.
Trains Depart				
From ABOYNE	...	7·50	11·0	7·0
From BANCHORY	7·25	8·50	12·10	8·10
Arrive at ABERDEEN about.........	9·0	9·50	1·30	9·15

For further information as to the Arrivals and Departures of Passenger Trains, Coaches running in connection, and Fares—see the Company's Time Table Books.

By order,

W. B. FERGUSON, Manager.

Deeside Railway Company's Offices,
Aberdeen, 29th November, 1859.

The announcement of the opening of the Aboyne extension in 1859.

which suffered from poor train timings: it was endemic throughout the Great North until the appointment 1879 of William Ferguson as chairman, followed the next year by the arrival of William Moffat from the North Eastern Railway as general manager. Between them they shook the Great North by the proverbial heels, changing it from one of the worst railways in the country into one of the best.

In 1880 the 4.30pm down and 8.08am up Ballater trains had their timing cut to 1½ hours with four intermediate stops and became known as the "Deeside Express". Ten years later the service varied at three or four trains timed to give an average of 95 minutes, with another going as far as Banchory.

By then more and more houses were being built between Aberdeen and Culter leading to the demand for a local train service, but this had to await the doubling of the track from Aberdeen, work which reached Culter in 1892. Two years later all was ready for the introduction of the Deeside 'Subbies', in connection with which new stations were opened that year at Holburn Street, Pitfodels and West Cults, with Bieldside following in 1897. These trains, and

OCTOBER, 1922.

GREAT NORTH OF SCOTLAND RAILWAY. 15

Between Aberdeen, Banchory, Aboyne, Ballater, &c.

Trains leave																	
	p.m.	p.m.	a.m.	a.m.	a.m.		a.m.	a.m.	p.m.			a.m.	p.m.				
London (Euston)	....	7§30	....	....	11 †0	....	....	....	....	....	....	....	....	....	....	....	....
Do. (St. Pancras)	....	....	....	9†15	....	....	....	....	....	....	....	....	....	....	....	....	....
Do. (King's Cross)	7‡30	....	....	10†20	....	....	....	....	....	....	....	4 45	....	....	....	....	....
Do. (Liverpool St.)	....	....	....	....	....	....	....	....	....	....	....	....	....	....	....	....	....
Edinbro' (via Stirling)	....	....	....	....	6a45	....	....	9 25	....	....	....	....	1 15	....	....	....	....
Do. (via Forth and Tay Bridges)	4a12	....	....	7 40a	....	....	10-25	....	....	....	....	2p30	....	....	....	....	....
Glasgow (Buch. St.)	....	....	4*15	....	7 15	....	....	10 0	....	....	....	....	1 30	....	....	....	....
Do. (Queen St.)	....	....	....	....	....	....	8 47	....	....	....	....	12 34	....	....	....	....	....
Perth	....	5a41	6 13	....	9 22	....	....	11 43	12 15	....	....	....	3 30	....	....	....	....
Aberdeen ......arrive	7 30	7 40	7 52	11 24	11 50	....	1p49	2p5	3 56	....	....	5 40	6 0	....	....	....	....

Miles	STATIONS	1	2	3	4	5	6	7	8	9	10	11	12	13	14	15	16	
					Not Sats	Sats only												
		a.m.		a.m.	p.m.	p.m.		p.m.		p.m.				p.m.	p.m.			
....	Aberdeen ...depart	8 5	....	10 10	1 0	1 25	....	3 20	....	4 40	....	....	....	6 15	6 50	....	....	....
1¼	Holburn Street	....	....	....	....	....	....	....	....	....	....	....	....	....	6 54	....	....	....
1¾	Ruthrieston	....	....	....	....	....	....	....	....	....	....	....	....	....	6 56	....	....	....
3	Pitfodels	....	....	....	....	....	....	....	....	....	....	....	....	....	....	....	....	....
3¾	Cults	....	....	10 18	....	1 43	....	....	....	....	....	....	....	....	7 2	....	....	....
4¼	West Cults	....	....	....	....	....	....	....	....	....	....	....	....	....	7 4	....	....	....
4¾	Bieldside	....	....	....	....	1 46	....	....	....	....	....	....	....	....	7 6	....	....	....
5¾	Murtle	....	....	a	....	....	....	....	....	....	....	....	....	....	7 9	....	....	....
6¼	Milltimber	....	....	a	....	....	....	....	....	....	....	....	....	....	7 12	....	....	....
7¼	Culter	8 19	....	10 26	1 14	1 53	....	3 34	....	4 54	....	....	....	6 29	7 16	....	....	....
9¼	Drum	8 25	....	10 32	1 20	1 59	....	3 40	....	5 0	....	....	....	6 35	7 22	....	....	....
10¾	Park	8 28	....	10 35	1 23	2 2	....	3 43	....	5 3	....	....	....	6 38	7 25	....	....	....
14½	Crathes	8 34	....	10 41	1 29	2 8	....	3 49	....	5 9	....	....	....	6 44	7 32	....	....	....
16¾	Banchery	8 43	....	10 49	1 35	2 14	....	3 58	....	5 15	....	....	....	6 51	7 39	....	....	....
21¼	Glassel	8 53	....	10 59	stop	stop	....	4 8	....	stop	....	....	....	7 1	Stop.	....	....	....
23¾	Torphins	9 0	....	11 4	....	....	....	4 16	....	....	....	....	....	7 7	....	....	....	....
26¼	Lumphanan	9 8	....	11 12	....	....	....	4 24	....	....	....	....	....	7 15	....	....	....	....
29¼	Dess	9 13	....	11 17	....	....	....	4 29	....	....	....	....	....	7 20	....	....	....	....
32¼	Aboyne	9 20	....	11 24	....	....	....	4 36	....	....	....	....	....	7 28	....	....	....	....
36¾	Dinnet	9 30	....	11 35	....	....	....	4 45	....	....	....	....	....	7 38	....	....	....	....
39¾	Cambus O' May	9 37	....	11 42	....	....	....	4 52	....	....	....	....	....	7 45	....	....	....	....
43¼	Ballater ...arrive	9 45	....	11 50	....	....	....	5 0	....	....	....	....	....	7 53	....	....	....	....

Miles	STATIONS	1	2	3	4	5	6	7	8	9	10	11	12	13	14	15	16	17
		a.m.		a.m.			a.m.			p.m.		p.m.		p.m.		p.m.		
....	Ballater ......dep.	....	....	7 50	....	....	9 55	....	....	....	....	3 35	....	....	....	6 25	....	....
3½	Cambus O' May	....	....	7 57	....	....	10 2	....	....	....	....	3 42	....	....	....	6 32	....	....
6½	Dinnet	....	....	8 2	....	....	10 8	....	....	....	....	3 48	....	....	....	6 38	....	....
11	Aboyne	....	....	8 10	....	....	10 16	....	....	....	....	3 56	....	....	....	6 46	....	....
13¾	Dess	....	....	8 16	....	....	10 22	....	....	....	....	4 2	....	....	....	6 52	....	....
16¾	Lumphanan	....	....	8 22	....	....	10 28	....	....	....	....	4 8	....	....	....	6 58	....	....
19¼	Torphins	....	....	8 28	....	....	10 35	....	....	....	....	4 16	....	....	....	7 7	....	....
21¾	Glassel	....	....	8 33	....	....	10 40	....	....	....	....	4 21	....	....	....	7 12	....	....
26½	Banchery	7 48	....	8 45	....	....	10 52	....	....	2 35	....	4 33	....	5 48	....	7 26	....	....
29	Crathes	7 54	....	8 51	....	....	10 58	....	....	2 41	....	4 39	....	5 54	....	7 33	....	....
32½	Park	8 1	....	8 57	....	....	11 5	....	....	2 47	....	4 46	....	6 0	....	7 40	....	....
33¾	Drum	8 4	....	9 0	....	....	11 8	....	....	2 50	....	4 49	....	6 3	....	7 43	....	....
35½	Culter	8 9	....	9 5	....	....	11 13	....	....	2 55	....	4 54	....	6 8	....	7 48	....	....
37	Milltimber	....	....	....	....	....	....	....	....	....	....	....	....	....	....	....	....	....
37½	Murtle	....	....	....	....	....	....	....	....	....	....	....	....	....	....	....	....	....
38½	Bieldside	....	....	....	....	....	....	....	....	....	....	....	....	....	....	....	....	....
39	West Cults	....	....	....	....	....	....	....	....	....	....	....	....	....	....	....	....	....
39½	Cults	8 13	....	....	....	....	....	....	....	....	....	....	....	....	....	....	....	....
40¼	Pitfodels	....	....	....	....	....	....	....	....	....	....	....	....	....	....	....	....	....
41½	Ruthrieston	....	....	....	....	....	....	....	....	....	....	....	....	....	....	....	....	....
41¾	Holburn Street	....	....	....	....	....	....	....	....	....	....	....	....	....	....	....	....	....
43¼	Aberdeen ......arr.	8 30	....	9 20	....	....	11 30	....	....	3 10	....	5 10	....	6 25	....	8 5	....	....

		a.m.	a.m.	a.m.	p.m.	p.m.		p.m.	p.m.	p.m.	p.m.	p.m.	p.m.		a.m.	a.m.	
Aberdeen ......dep.	....	9 50	10 5	10 15	12 30	12 50	....	3 25	3 35	5 30	5 45	7 15	7¶30	....	6 15	6 30	....
Perth ......arr.	....	....	12p11	1p34	2 59	....	....	5 17	....	7 48	....	....	9¶35	....	....	8 40	....
Edinburgh (via Stirling)	....	....	2 22	4 46	6d54	....	....	7 35	....	10 0	....	....	....	....	....	11 7	....
Do. (via Tay and Forth Bridges)	....	1p19	....	....	....	4 33	....	....	7 21	....	9 17	10 26	12*7	....	9 42	....	....
Glasgow (Buch. St.)	....	....	2 20	4 20	4 55	....	....	7 15	....	9*50	....	....	....	....	....	10 33	....
Do. (Queen St.)	....	....	....	....	....	6 2	....	....	9 48	....	....	....	....	....	....	....	....
London (Liverpool St.)	....	....	....	....	....	....	....	....	....	....	....	....	....	....	....	....	....
Do. (King's Cross)	....	10 10	....	....	....	3a25	....	....	6a0	....	7a30	7a35	....	....	6p30	....	....
Do. (St. Pancras)	....	....	....	....	....	....	....	....	....	....	8a3	....	....	....	7p55	....	....
Do. (Euston)	....	....	10 30	....	5a0	....	....	....	....	....	....	....	8c0	....	....	7p30	....

a Stops to lift Passengers for West of Culter on timeous notice being given to the Station master.
c 8-20 a.m. on Sundays.
§ Not on Sats.—7-40 p.m. on Sundays. * Glasgow (Central Station). † Also runs on Sundays. ‡ Not on Saturdays.
¶ On Saturdays leaves Aberdeen at 7-45 p.m. and Perth at 9-50 p.m.
d Waverley Station.

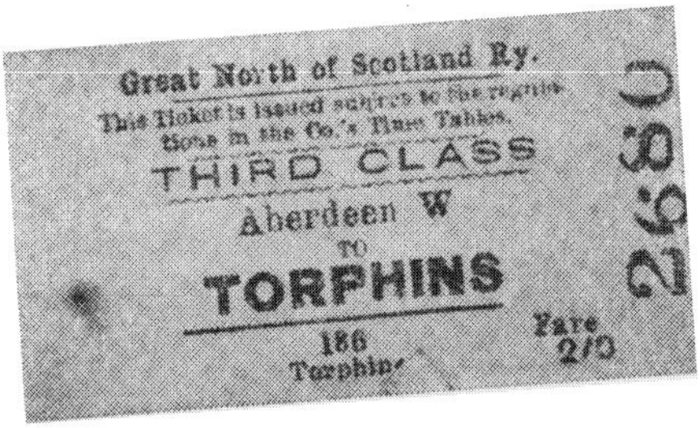

The winter timetable of 1922 was the final one issued by the GNSR before its absorption into the new London & North Eastern Railway.

The first Sunday 'Subby' waits to leave Culter on 3rd June 1928. The carriages are ex-Great Eastern six wheelers.

their counterparts out to Dyce, on the main line to Elgin, were quite remark-able. They were timed to cover the $7^1/_2$ miles to Culter in 21 minutes including eight intermediate stops. Even to-day's diesel and electric trains with centrally controlled sliding doors are hard pushed to beat these times by steam hauled trains with old-fashioned slam door carriages.

The Deeside service peaked in Summer 1914 when there were no less than seven Ballater trains with an extra on Wednesdays and Saturdays, giving an average journey time of 95 minutes. A further four ran to Banchory, again with extras — two on Wednesdays and Saturdays with a late evening departure from Aberdeen on Saturdays only. That timetable saw an interesting development when the down Deeside Express, now allowed 65 minutes to Ballater stopping only at Torphins and Aboyne, dropped off two slip-coaches at Banchory. This was a method of providing a service at a station without the train having to stop, the guard using a special mechanism to uncouple the slip coaches from the moving train. The service was short-lived as the Great War intervened and it was not reinstated afterwards. Incidentally this is believed to be the only example of a slip-coach operation on a standard gauge single track line.

During the 1914-18 war Banchory lost one of its trains while only four ran through to Ballater, one of the casualties being the Express, with the

Table 214   ABERDEEN, CULTER, BANCHORY, and BALLATER

Miles from Aberdeen		Week Days only							Miles		Week Days only			
		p.m	p.m	a.m	a.m	p.m E	p.m S				a.m	a.m	p.m	p.m
1	London(King'sC.) dp	7b50	7t30	..	1 0	..	..	—	Ballater .... dap		7 15	1015	3 26	5 54
184	EDINBURGH(Way.)	3a40	4 L 8	..	10 0	2 15	2 15	2¾	Cambus O'May		7 22	1022	3 33	6 1
184	GLASGOW (Q.St.)	..	..	8 47	12 50	1250		6½	Dinnet		7 27	1027	3 38	6 6
—	Aberdeen .... dep	8 5	19 0	3p10	6 15	6 50		11	Aboyne		7 30	1036	3 48	6 15
3¼	Cults	8 14	10 9	3 19	6 24	6 59		13½	Dess		7 42	1042	3 54	6 21
7¼	Culter	8 22	10 17	3 27	6 32	7 7		16½	Lumphanan		7 49	1050	4 2	6 28
9¼	Drum	..	10 23	3 33	..	..		19½	Torphins		7 56	1059	4 10	6 35
10¾	Park	8 29	10 26	8 36	6 39	7 14		21½	Glassel		8 1	11 4	4 15	6 40
14	Crathes	8 35	10 32	8 42	6 45	7 20		26¼	Banchory		8 10	1113	4 24	6 51
17	Banchory	8 42	10 39	3 49	6 52	7 27		29½	Crathes		8 16	1119	4 30	6 57
21½	Glassel	8 53	10 50	4 0	7 3	7 38		32½	Park		8 22	1125	4 36	7 3
23¾	Torphins	9 0	10 59	4 10	7 10	7 45		33½	Drum		8 25	1128	4 39	..
27	Lumphanan	9 8	11 7	4 18	7 18	7 53		35½	Culter		8 30	1133	4 44	7 9
29½	Dess	9 13	11 12	4 23	7 23	7 58		39½	Cults		8 37	1140	4 51	7 16
32¼	Aboyne	9 19	11 18	4 29	7 29	8 5	43¼		Aberdeen .... arr		8 46	1149	5 0	7 25
36½	Dinnet	9 29	11 28	4 39	7 39	8 15	203½	184	GLASGOW (Q. St.) arr		..	5p55	..	1015
39½	Cambus O'May	9 35	11 34	4 45	7 45	8 21	173½	184	EDINBURGH(Way.)		1p20	4 25	..	9 15
43¼	Ballater L .... arr	9 42	11 41	4 52	7 52	8 28	566½	1	London(King'sC.)		10 5	5a 5	..	4a20

a a.m.   *l* Applies on Weekdays (except Saturdays) and Sundays   **E** Except Saturdays
L Station for Balmoral and Braemar   .   Monday and Saturday mornings only   **P** Limited Sleeping
accommodation between King's Cross and Aberdeen   *p* p.m.   **S** Saturdays only   *t* Friday and Sunday nights only

The last LNER timetable: winter 1947.

Wednesday and Saturday trains being withdrawn completely. After the war the Express was re-instated in 1920 but the others did not re-appear.

In 1928 the LNER introduced Sunday trains, mainly 'Subbies' to Culter but during the Summer months three trains went to Banchory with a fourth going through to Ballater and these survived until the outbreak of war but were never restored thereafter. Sadly the 'Subbies' succumbed to bus competition and were withdrawn on 5th April 1937.

By September 1939 there were only four trains left, all of them going to Ballater in around 1hr 40 minutes calling at every station, and for the duration of the war they had to suffice despite the lack of fuel for cars and buses. Not only had freight traffic increased from around 46,000 tons in 1940 to over 175,000 tons three years later but the line had to handle all the extra trains arising from the presence of the many army units stationed along Deeside. Staff and equipment were stretched to the limit.

After the return of peace matters gradually improved and eventually the pattern settled down to six trains each way in Summer with one less in Winter.

A big change occurred on 21st April 1958 when steam gave way to its modern successors. In this case the normal diesel railcars

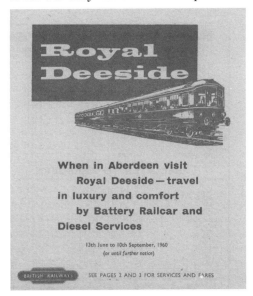

Table 40   **ABERDEEN and BALLATER**

Week Days only

Miles		am				am				pm E	pm S			pm		pm		Runs until 8th October, 1964 and from 26th April, 1965	pm	Runs 9th October, 1964 to 24th April, 1965	pm F
—	Aberdeen ... ... dep	8 9	..	..	..	9 38	..	..	..	1 55	1 55	..	..	3 45	..	6 10	..		8 35		8 35
3½	Cults	8 17	..			9 46	..		..					3 53		6 18	..				
7½	Culter	8 27	..			9 53	..			2 8	2 8		..	4 0	..	6 25	..				
10¾	Park	8 34	..			10 0	..			2 15	2 15			4 7		6 32	..				
14	Crathes	8 39	..			10 5	..							4 12							
17	Banchory	8 45	..			10 11	..		..	2 25	2 25		..	4 22		6 42	..	9 10		9 10	
17½	Dee Street Halt.. ...	8 47	..			10 13	..			2 27	2 27		..	4 24		6 44	..	9 12		9 12	
21½	Glassel	8 56	..			10 22	..			2K36	2 36		..	4 33	..	6 53	..	9K20		9K20	
13½	Torphins	9 1	..			10 27	..			2 41	2 41		..	4 38	..	6 58	..	9 25		9 25	
27	Lumphanan	9 8	..			10 34	..			2 48	2 48		..	4 45	..	7 5	..	9 32		9 32	
29½	Dess	9 12	..			10 38	..				2 52		..	4 49	..	7 9	..				
32½	Aboyne	9 17	..			10 43	..			2 56	2 57		..	4 54	..	7 14	..	9 40		9 40	
36½	Dinnet	9 25	..			10 51	..			3 4	3 5		..	5 2	..	7 22	..	9 48		9 48	
39½	Cambus o'May Halt	9K31	..			10K57	..									7K28	..				
43½	Ballater ... ... arr	9 37	..			11 3	..			3 14	3 15		..	5 12	..	7 34	..	9 58		9 58	

Week Days only

Miles		am				am				pm				pm		pm		Runs 9th October, 1964 to 24th April, 1965	pm F	Runs until 8th October, 1964 and from 26th April, 1965	pm
—	Ballater ... ... dep	7 20	..			10 3	..			12 30	..		..	3 25	..	5 33	..		8 3		8 3
3½	Cambus o'May Halt	7K27	..			10K10	..			12K37	..		..	3K32	..		..		8 13		8 13
7	Dinnet	7 31	..			10 14	..			12 41	..		..	3 36	..	5 43	..		8 20		8 20
11	Aboyne	7 38	..			10 21	..			12 48	..		..	3 43	..	5 50	..				
13½	Dess	7 43	..			10 26	..			12 53	..		..	3 48	..		..		8 30		8 30
16½	Lumphanan	7 48	..			10K36	..			12 58	..		..	3 53	..	6 0	..		8 37		8 37
19½	Torphins	7 55	..			10 43	..			1 5	..		..	0 0	..	6 7	..				
21½	Glassel	8 0	..			10 48	..			1K10	..		..	4 5	..	6 12	..				
25½	Dee Street Halt.. ...	8 7	..			10 55	..			1 17	..		..	4 12	..	6 19	..		8 47		8 47
26	Banchory	8 9	..			10 57	..			1 19	..		..	4C20	..	6 21	..		8 49		8 49
29½	Crathes	8 14	..			11 2	..				..		..	4 25	..		..				
32½	Park	8 19	..			11 7	..			1 28	..		..	4 30	..	6 33	..		9 3		9 3
35½	Culter	8 25	..			11 13	..			1 34	..		..	4 36	..	6 39	..				
39½	Cults	8 31	..			11 19	..				..		..	4 42	..		..				
43½	Aberdeen ... ... arr	8 39	..			11 27	..			1 46	..		..	4 50	..	6 51	..		9 15		9 15

C Arr 6 minutes earlier	K Calls to set down on request to guard	S Saturdays only
E Except Saturdays	or when there are passengers to be	
F Fridays and Saturdays only	taken up	

The winter 1964 timetable shows the final pattern of services on the Deeside line.

were supplemented by the unique battery railcar. The service pattern remained the same but with an improved journey time of around 1hr 20 minutes, the timetable remaining virtually unchanged until all services were withdrawn on 28th February 1966.

The last passenger service to Ballater was the 8.35pm on Saturday 28th February, 1966. Here it is almost ready to pull out of the Joint Station. (courtesy Aberdeen Journals)

DEESIDE RAILWAY.

PLEASURE TRIP to UPPER BANCHORY, under the auspices of the ABERDEEN TEMPERANCE SOCIETY, on WEDNESDAY first, 14th curt. Fares to Banchory and back One Shilling, Third Class; One and Sixpence, First Class. The Train will leave Ferryhill Station, at Eleven, A.M., and Banchory at 6·30, P.M.

Members of the above Society, and others friendly to its objects, may obtain Tickets from Messrs. GEORGE MAITLAND, 40, Broad Street; JOHN M'DONALD, Confectioner, Market Buildings; JOHN M'QUARRIE, Clothier, Correction Wynd; WILLIAM LINDSAY, Book-seller, Gallowgate; GEORGE HENRY, Bookseller, Broad Street; and at the Deeside Railway Office.

W. B. FERGUSON, Manager.

Aberdeen 10th Sept., 1853.

High days and holidays

It was always expected that excursion and holiday traffic would feature large in the life of the Deeside line. Two days after it opened the company announced that "a TRAIN of FIRST-CLASS CARRIAGES" would run non-stop to and from Banchory on the following Tuesday. The next day the Aberdeen Temperance Society arranged "A Pleasure Trip to Upper Banchory". This was not a special train but the fares were only valid on the 11am down and 6.30pm up trains. By the end of the month cheap fares were available on Saturdays for return that day or the following Monday. So began what was to become a feature of the railway's work.

The annual Aberdeen holidays gave many opportunities for special trains and fares. The first of these came with the July 1854 holiday when excursion tickets were issued to all stations. "56 carriages took 1,700 along the beautiful route of the Deeside line — for the most part to Banchory". Twenty years later summer traffic was clearly causing problems for the Great North which worked the line on behalf of the Deeside Railway and this led to an official complaint from the Company. "Some trains in summer are now so large that neither the platforms or sidings are at all adequate for them, and there is often risk of accidents arising from such a state of affairs." The need to finance improvements was one of the reasons for the amalgamation of the two Companies.

Special trains and fares were not confined to peak holiday times. When the railway had been opened to Aboyne, excursion tickets were available on 8th August 1860 to allow visitors to witness the arrival of Queen Victoria on her way to Balmoral. They would also be run for such events as the Highland Games at Aboyne and the Braemar Gathering, to say nothing of those operated into Aberdeen for the Royal Northern Show, football matches or theatrical events for which the railway would even book seats for travellers.

Trains run in connection with the Aberdeen Spring Holiday in 1899 give a good idea of the numbers involved. To quote the *Aberdeen Journal:* "*Deeside was as usual a very popular resort, most of the trains taking large numbers of excursionists. For stations from Drum to Ballater there was a fair run, about 350 excursionists leaving on a special at 7am. Less than half that number travelled on the ordinary train at 8.5. The most popular train was the 8.45 which connects at Ballater with the coach route to Crathie. About 550 passengers took advantage of this train. An hour later about 200 excursionists went to Banchory and at 10.20 the train with passengers from Cults to Banchory lifted about 450 excursionists. Still better was the excursion that left at 11am for the same destinations, about 500 passengers going by that train. At 11.25 about 400 passengers travelled, although other Deeside trains were not so well filled, about1100 left between 11.55am and 1.45pm, 300 going at 11.55, 200 at 12.20 and 300 each at 12.45 and 1.45*".

To cope with all the extra passengers older vehicles which spent most of their time in sidings throughout the system were collected and sent to Aberdeen. As some of the original Deeside carriages lasted until the early 1920s, the passengers must have had a fairly rough ride!

The Great North always regarded the Deeside Line as one of its main tourist attractions and gave it wide publicity. As an added interest to the journey, in 1918 the height of the line above sea level was shown on the station name boards from Banchory onwards. This caught the attention of the LNER directors when they visited Deeside in 1925 so the idea was extended to their other lines in Scotland with tourist traffic.

After 1919 the pressures slowly began to decline with the advent of cars and buses. Even so the trains still provided the best means of moving large

Ballater during Aberdeen holiday week, 1959. The battery rail-car formed the 5.35pm, while BR Class 4 No.76104 heads a relief train leaving 15 minutes later. (The late Roy Hamilton)

The pupils from Kelman Memorial Church Sunday School, Culter, wait at Torphins to board their return excursion train after their annual picnic in the local park. The train is double headed with two BR tank engines.

numbers on special occasions. For example on Saturday 16th June 1926 no less than 3,285 people made up from eleven Sunday School parties went to Pitfodels, Murtle, Milltimber and Culter. They travelled in three special trains which left Aberdeen between 1.53pm and 2.22pm with the regular 2.05 'Subby' also running. Unloading at the various stations must have been slick! This traffic continued, although on a reducing scale, into the 1950s. Saturday 27th June 1953 saw Sunday School specials at 1.30pm to Park, always a popular destination, and half an hour later to Crathes and Banchory.

Holiday makers were also catered for in other ways. By using their buses in connection with the normal train services the GNSR offered a couple of interesting tours based on Deeside. The first venture, the 'Three Rivers Tour', started on 1st July 1907 and was a two-day affair. Passengers left Aberdeen by the 8.05am train for Dinnet where they joined a char-a-banc which took them to Cockbridge. The road on to Tomintoul, crossing The Lecht at some 2,100 feet, was considered too steep for motor vehicles so they transferred to a horse-drawn coach. After spending the night at Tomintoul they continued,

In 1910, The GNSR produced this 16 page illustrated booklet advertising the scenic beauties of the Three Rivers Tours.

again by char-a-banc, to Ballindalloch and completed the journey back to Aberdeen via the Speyside Line and Keith. All this for a fare of 20/- First Class or 15/- Third Class. Through fares could even be booked from Edinburgh and Glasgow.

About three years later a shortened version was introduced — the 'Two Rivers Tour'. This took participants from Dinnet via Strathdon to Alford for return by train to Aberdeen.

When war broke out in 1914 the 'Two Rivers' continued but the 'Three Rivers' was suspended for the duration being resumed in 1919, but their popularity waned and they did not survive into LNER days.

In 1933 the LNER introduced the concept of Camping Coaches at several holiday resorts in England. These coaches were converted from old vehicles and normally provided accommodation for 4 to 6 people. Conditions were fairly primitive by present day standards — cooking and lighting were done using paraffin, with toilet facilities normally in the station buildings. Even so they proved very popular and in 1935 they appeared on Deeside, being placed at Murtle, Crathes, Banchory and Cambus O'May and subsequently at Torphins, Aboyne and Ballater. Banchory in particular proved so popular that a second coach was located there. After the war, people's expectations changed and only Aboyne had one from 1955 until 1960. A final development, which lasted about 10 years, was the provision of Camping Apartments within the station building at Banchory.

The 'Glendee Restaurant' was at the front of Ballater Station. An undated leaflet issued by British Transport Catering Services is worth quoting:

"True, it is on a railway station, but don't let that alarm you! In the mahogany-panelled dining room or the extension, with its gaily patterned contemporary decorations, excellently cooked meals are served. From the illustrations you can form an idea of the surroundings and from the specimen menus you can judge the type of repast you will enjoy. Look particularly at the prices. No attempt is made to provide exotic dishes. What you will get is plain, good cooking — the kind you like at home...."

The 6/- Luncheon could include tomato soup; fried fillet of haddock; hot roast beef; steak & kidney pie; cold boiled ham & salad; fruit tart; jelly & ice cream. High tea was 5/- with the bonus of 'chip potatoes' with your bacon and egg.

On her way from Ballater station to Balmoral in September 1897, Queen Victoria passes the flag-bedecked Memorial Hall named after her beloved Albert. (*Aberdeen University Library, G.W. Wilson Collection*)

Royal Train journeys

In 1848 Balmoral was leased by the Royal family. Three years later Prince Albert bought it and gave it to Queen Victoria who in turn left it as a holiday residence for future sovereigns, thus beginning an association between the royal family and the Deeside line which continued throughout its existence. The Queen's mother, the Duchess of Kent, became the first royal passenger when she went south from Banchory on 11th October 1853, just over a month after the railway opened. Two days later the Queen herself, accompanied by Prince Albert and their family, travelled to London. The weather had been very bad making movement by road difficult and tedious. Consequently the royal party was 25 minutes late in arriving at Banchory where a triumphal arch surmounted by a golden crown had been erected at the entrance to the station, as well as the customary red carpet on the platform. On her way south the following year she "desired to have luncheon at Banchory station" and arrangements were made with Mr Grant, of the Burnett Arms Hotel, to provide the food. When the same request came the following year Mr Grant again catered but the Company arranged to keep down the cost of decorations. From then on journeys by British and foreign royalty brought a good deal of traffic to the line.

As the railway was extended, these journeys ran to and from Aboyne and then Ballater: indeed the royal train used the final length the day before it was officially opened, and thereby hangs a tale. When Captain Tyler inspected the line for the Board of Trade he was not satisfied with the safety of a couple of bridges and ordered further work including temporarily propping up the girders pending their replacement. He then wrote to Sir Stafford Northcote (apparently a member of the royal household) telling him what he had done, adding *"I think it is right to tell you of this. If you should hear of a bridge being propped up you will know the reason. But you need not be under any apprehension as regards the Queen's going over the line on Tuesday, and it may still be opened as proposed for public traffic on Wednesday."*

The original station at Ballater was a rather mean little place, which may be the reason the Queen continued to use Aboyne for almost a year after it was opened. Its shortcomings led Mr McKenzie of Glenmuick to write privately and personally in 1884 to William Ferguson, the chairman of the GNSR, suggesting that a Royal waiting room would be appreciated:

"The expense could only be a trifle for making a small room of the kind required, and it would appear as a kindly offer of respect coming unsolicited from the Railway. Should the Railway not have the funds to do so, I have no doubt other Railways drawing advantage from the traffic would gladly contribute although I think you will agree with me that it would look better coming from the Deeside (sic) Railway alone if you could manage it, and for this reason I make this letter private to you, that if done it should appear to be the spontaneous action of the Railway".

This prompted (or should it be shamed?) the directors into taking action and they approved its re-building. The plans included a Royal waiting room modelled on that at Wolferton, the station for Sandringham. The new station was opened in 1886 and when Queen Victoria arrived on Saturday 21st August of that year she inspected, and duly approved, the accommodation provided for her.

Queen Victoria nearly always travelled by the West Coast route and in 1869 the London and North Western Railway, as the senior partner, built a pair of six-wheeled saloons connected to each other (but not to the rest of the train) by a gangway. It was not until 1895 that the Queen allowed them to be partially rebuilt by being joined together and mounted on a pair of bogies. Even so, during the whole of her reign there were no vestibule connections with the rest of the train. As steps were only provided on the royal carriage, this created difficulties for those attending her. If their services were dispensed with at some isolated spot where no platform existed, her ladies had to climb back aboard their own carriages as best they could, using only the footboards — dark nights, wind and rain not withstanding! It was not until King Edward VII ascended the throne that the LNWR was able to provide the magnificent new train which appeared in 1903 and lasted until 1941, when it was superseded by one built in the LMSR works at Wolverton which in its turn was replaced in the late 1970s.

HM King Edward VII at Ballater station.

The GNSR Royal Train in September 1903, the date showing that it is almost certainly the one used by King Edward VII when he came north that year after attending Doncaster races.

The third coach is GNSR First Class Saloon No.1 'the Royal Saloon', shortly to be restored at the Scottish Railway Preservation Society Museum at Bo'ness.

Immediate & Important.

TELEGRAMS—
"DEUCHAR, RAILWAY, ABERDEEN."

TELEPHONE
Nº 366.

Great North of Scotland Railway,
Passenger Superintendent's Office,
Aberdeen 14th August, 1913.

S.-
Refer to
P.13/4597.

Mr. Grant,

    Ballater.

Dear Sir,

       Journey of Her Majesty The Queen, Euston to Ballater,
          Thursday, 14th August.

     I am now advised that Royal Train to-day consists of 9

vehicles, and that the distance from front buffer of leading vehicle

on arrival at Ballater to centre of door-way of Royal Saloon

is 379 feet 2 inches, and total length of train over all is 548 feet

6 inches. *I have asked Engineer to indicate the exact*

point of stoppage at Ballater by a signal opposite

to where the front Yours truly, *buffer of leading vehicle*

should come to a stand.

        W. Deuchar

It was not only members of our own royal family that visited Deeside. In July 1889 His Imperial Majesty the Shah of Persia stayed at both Balmoral and Invercauld. On his return from the latter somebody made a serious mistake in calculating the time taken to reach Ballater so that he arrived forty minutes early. No one was ready and even the Guard of Honour had not appeared. The royal party therefore sat in the train until the soldiers arrived and were duly inspected.

Seven years later Nicholas II, Czar of all the Russians, visited the Queen, the Czarina being her granddaughter. The Czar was not a popular visitor to this country being "a political personage whose unlimited power exceeds that of any other monarch on earth" and in any event Russia was not well liked in this country and special security arrangements were in force all along the line. Despite this, Ballater station was extravagantly decorated and lit by electricity especially installed to light not only the station itself but also the square outside and even the road as far as the burgh boundary. Some royal families spurned pomp and circumstance and travelled to and from Balmoral incognito — notably the Kings of Belgium and Portugal.

Queen Victoria's last journey took place on 7th November 1900. At her own request it was a private occasion with no one on the platform to see her off. Little more than two months later she died.

During the reign of King Edward VII the Great North provided a royal train from its own stock on at least ten occasions, and indeed it was the only pre-Grouping Scottish railway to have a royal saloon. This still exists at the railway museum at Bo'ness. These trains were mainly for private visits such as the occasions when the Prince of Wales stayed with friends on Speyside, or Queen Alexandra went to Dundee on her way to visit her family in Denmark. September 1903, however, was altogether different. The Great Northern Railway asked the GNSR to provide a train to take the King from London to Ollerton where he spent two days attending the races at Doncaster before going north to Ballater. Needless to say the company made the most of this, even claiming that the "King commanded the use of the Royal train". The last royal train provided by the Company ran on 19th September 1910 for Queen Alexandra who by then was the Queen Mother.

Since that time there have been many royal trains and, like their pre-decessors, each involved a good deal of work for all concerned. Normally a pilot engine was run ten or fifteen minutes in advance of the royal train, and after its passage all the trains that would be passed by it were stopped. The track was closely guarded and all level crossing gates closed and locked. At one time, because of the Fenian outrages, concern was felt

On a pre-war visit, HM King George VI inspects the Guard of Honour before leaving Ballater station for Balmoral.

for Queen Victoria's safety, and men were posted in sight of each other along the whole route from Windsor to Ballater. On Deeside at least this precaution was continued until 1923. Over the years however, several of these special restrictions have been relaxed, but even so, the greatest care is taken in running a Royal train.

Full details of its movements would be contained in special and confidential notices issued to, and signed for, by everybody concerned. The notice would include precise instructions regarding the running of both it and other trains on the route, security arrangements at points and level crossings and, not least, ensuring that the train stopped at the exact place where the red carpet had been laid! (see letter on page 33)

One of the most detailed notices related to Queen Victoria's journey from Gosport to Ballater in August 1887. (See following pages). For this, covering 623 miles, there are no less than 195 timing points. The train consisted of 15 vehicles, seven on either side of the royal saloon. Leaving Gosport at 6.50pm on 24th August there were stops at Basingstoke, Banbury (reached at 10.01pm where 15 minutes were allowed for refreshments), Bushbury, and Wigan. Oxenholme saw a stop presumably to attach a banking engine to assist with the climbs over Greyrigg and Shap. Further stops were made at Carlisle, Beattock Summit and Larbert before reaching Perth at 9.34am where 55 minutes were allowed for breakfast. Then came a five minute stop at Bridge of Dun with another five minutes at Aberdeen before the train finally reached Ballater at 2.35pm. Unusually, the timetable even includes a gradient diagram of the whole route.

The final royal train on Deeside left Ballater at 7.15pm on 15th October 1965 hauled by two diesel engines. As with the first journey by a Monarch, and indeed the day of Queen Elizabeth's first arrival on 8th August 1952, the weather was bad with a steady downpour of rain. Even so a crowd of several hundred people bade her farewell.

As it turned out this was not to be the final royal visit to Ballater station. When the reigning King or Queen arrived by train it was usual for them to inspect the royal guard drawn up in the square outside. The last time this ceremony had taken place was in 1964 as in the following year Her Majesty arrived in Aberdeen by sea and then drove to Balmoral. Over the years since then there had been suggestions that the ceremony be revived. The committee of the Great North of Scotland Railway Association felt that 1986, being the centenary year of the royal waiting room, would provide a suitable opportunity. Her Majesty graciously approved the suggestion and so when she went to Balmoral on 16th August that year, arrangements were made for her car to arrive on the platform side of the station, just as though she had come by train. There she was met by the Lord Lieutenant of Aberdeenshire, Sir Maitland Mackie, accompanied by Mr Maurice Shand, the only surviving Ballater stationmaster. The Queen then moved out into the square where she inspected the royal guard drawn from the 1st Battalion the Black Watch before setting off for Balmoral.

The afternoon sun lights up Cambus O'May during May 1960.
(The late Roy Hamilton)

Royal train empty stock passing through Banchory. *(The late N. Forrest)*

*The last Deeside line passenger train about to leave Ballater
on the night of 28th February 1966. (Alex Forsyth)*

*Aboyne Station in the hands of the demolition contractor, 1970.
(The late N. Forrest)*

38

TIME TABLE

FOR

REGULATING THE PROGRESS OF THE TRAIN

TO CONVEY

HER MAJESTY

FROM

GOSPORT TO BALLATER,

VIA BUSHBURY JUNCTION, CARLISLE, AND ABERDEEN.

On WEDNESDAY, the 24th,

AND

THURSDAY, the 25th AUGUST, 1887.

McCORQUODALE & CO., LIMITED, CARDINGTON STREET, LONDON, N.W.

(Major F.C.Q. Irvine)

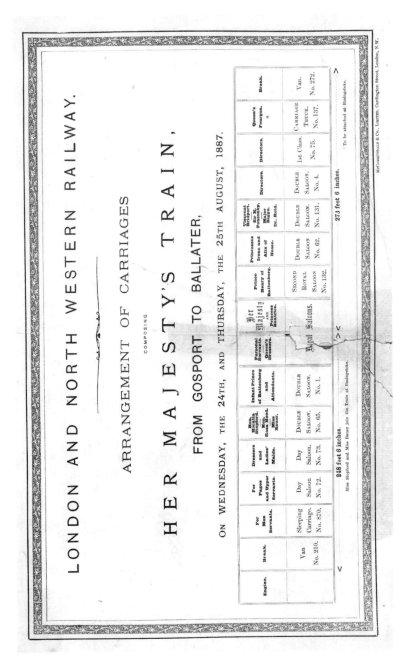

The train formation. The train lengths allowed officials to calculate where to lay the red carpet. (see letter on page 33). (Major F.C.Q. Irvine)

ABERDEEN	576¼	Cove ... ... „	12 58
	580½	**Aberdeen** ... ... arr.	P.M. 1 6
		„ ... ...dep.	1 11
	583⅓	Cults ... ... pass	1 17
	586½	Milltimber ... ... „	1 22
	587½	Culter ... ... „	1 24
	589¾	Drum ... ... „	1 29
BANCHORY	590¾	Park ... ... „	1 31
	596¾	Banchory ... ... „	1 42
	601¼	Glassel ... ... „	1 51
	603¾	Torphins ... ... „	1 56
	606¾	Lumphanan... ... „	2 2
ABOYNE	609½	Dess ... ... „	2 7
	612	Aboyne... ... ... „	2 13
	616½	Dinnet ... ... „	2 22
BALLATER	619	Cambus O'May ... „	2 27
	623	**Ballater** ... ... arr.	2 35

From the 1887 journey, showing the Deeside line. Note the gradient profile alongside. (Major F.C.Q. Irvine)

The Messenger trains

When Queen Victoria began to spend part of each year at Balmoral her despatches had perforce to be sent daily to and from London in the care of a Queen's Messenger. At first they came by road from Perth via Blairgowrie, the Cairnwell Pass and Braemar, but in 1864 the directors of the Deeside Railway reckoned they could convey the Messenger with advantage to their company. The secretary therefore wrote to the Queen's Private Secretary proposing special trains between Aberdeen and Aboyne running in connection with those to and from London. The company undertook to make the journey from Aberdeen to Balmoral in 3hrs 40mins, including 15 minutes at Aboyne for the transfer from train to carriage. This being duly agreed the first 'Messenger' ran on 8th Oc-

The Royal Train about to leave Ballater in August 1928, showing the magnificent set of coaches built by the erstwhile London & North Western Railway. The former Great North engines, Nos.6850 'Hatton Castle' and 6846 'Benachie' are beautifully turned out and are complete with the special Royal Train headcode of four white discs. (National Railway Museum)

tober 1865. Leaving Aberdeen at 4.0am, where it connected with the train which had left London the previous morning, it stopped only at Banchory and reached Aboyne at 5.25am.

To begin with the train was first-class only, though later on third-class accommodation was provided for the first-class passengers' servants. By the end of the century third-class passengers were also carried and eventually the trains appeared in the public timetable. They were unique in being the only ones on the Great North to run on the Sabbath.

The Treasury paid for the Messenger at a cost of £9:2/- for each return journey, including £1:1:6d to cover running the carriage and pair used to complete delivery to the castle. In 1887, however, it queried the cost, reckoning that the Great North was charging too much. After some discussion the Company agreed to reduce the charge to 1/6 per mile thus giving a saving of £1:11/- on rail charges each day the train ran, but the Treasury now had to pay for the 'posting' on to Balmoral.

As with most arrangements all did not always go according to plan. In 1924 the King's mail came north on the overnight LMS train from Euston which was due into Aberdeen at 7.40am, allowing 25 minutes for transfer to the 8.05 Ballater mail. That Autumn there was some terse correspondence about the fairly consistent late running of the former which was arriving anything up to 35 minutes behind time. Delaying the Ballater train led to problems with the Up Deeside train which had important connections at Aberdeen. In the end the Post Office, no doubt much to the LMS's chagrin, decided that on Sundays, which produced the worst problems, the King's mail would be sent care of the guard on an LNER train from King's Cross which, leaving London at the same time, was due in 10 minutes earlier.

By 1937 it was decided that road transport was sufficiently reliable to be able to dispense with the Messenger trains. Thus it was that in 1938 the despatches once again transferred to road at Perth and went north by the original route, which in any case was by then quicker, even though it was far from to-day's good road.

Running these trains led in part to a lawsuit in 1883. When Crathes station was opened in 1863 it was made a condition that all passenger trains would stop there. The Messengers however did not do so, the Company maintaining that because they were subsidised by the Treasury they were not passenger trains within "the meaning of the Act." By 1878 they were in the public timetable as, incidentally, was a Saturday-only excursion to Banchory. Neither of these stopped at Crathes so Sir Robert Burnett of Leys, who owned the estate, told the Great North it was in default of its obligations. The case dragged its way through the courts before finally ending up, seven years later, in the House of Lords where their Lordships ruled that the 'Messenger' would have to stop — but not the excursion as it was not available to passengers with ordinary tickets! After that all trains duly stopped, albeit only momentarily, until in 1914 Sir Robert's successor set aside the relevant clause in the Feu Charter.

GNSR No.51 was one of the engines supplied by Hawthorn of Leith for the Deeside Railway. Built in 1859 as Deeside No.5, it was withdrawn in 1876. The man on the footplate is almost certainly locomotive foreman Hugh Dean.

Locomotives

Four months before the Deeside Railway was due to open, the company's engineer, Mr Willet, inspected a pair of tank engines belonging to the Caledonian Railway and which were surplus to their needs. It turned out they were not suitable and an order was placed in June 1853 with Messrs Hawthorn of Leith for two of their 0-4-0 tank engines, although this was soon altered to a 0-4-2 layout to allow for greater stability and increased water capacity. They nearly did not come as, while they were being built, Thomas Bouch, later of Tay Bridge fame (notoriety?), offered to buy them at £100 over cost on behalf of clients — such was the demand for engines at the time. In the end, the first was delivered in March 1854, just in time to save the day when the Scottish Central ceased to work the trains.

Hawthorn delivered six of these sturdy 0-4-2s, the first two being tank engines, with the final one arriving in June 1866. A seventh had an interesting history. The Banffshire Railway was impressed by the Deeside's engines and ordered two for themselves. When that company was taken over by the GNSR in 1863 they naturally entered their stock but the following year one was sold to the Deeside Railway, only for it to return to the Great North when two years later it leased the smaller concern.

They served their owners well but even so an anonymous writer to *Engineering* had this to say about them:-

"On the occasions when the royal train goes over the line, the speed is higher than for ordinary traffic. We are certain that engines of this construction would not be considered safe for so fast trains on the main lines in the south of England, and we wish to ask whether they are reckoned perfectly safe for the

exceptionally high speeds upon the crooked and undulating line which occupies the distance between Aberdeen and Balmoral."

As the Deeside trains had an average speed of less than 20mph it is tempting to ask the meaning of "exceptionally high speed"!

There was also an eighth engine, a poor thing supplied in 1854 by Messrs Dodds & Co of Rotherham which no doubt the board regretted ever having purchased. It was very troublesome and seems to have done little work. In 1867 the directors tried to sell it for what it was worth, but there were no takers. Even that was not quite the end of the story as five years later the Great North realised it had never been included in the lease inventory and it was finally written off.

The Deeside engines must have looked very smart decked out in their dark blue livery with black lining, especially as they were kept in an immaculate condition, as is found in the instructions to the locomotive foreman. "I hope you will make it your pride to have all the Engines kept as clean and tidy as possible, all brass and copper work of every kind being kept bright." There are rumours, which cannot be confirmed, that engine No.2 carried a tartan livery for a while. The story is that it was delegated to work the first Queen's Messenger trains and for this duty was painted all over in Royal Stuart Dress tartan. If so, it would have presented quite a sight!

During its separate existence the Deeside maintained their engines and rolling stock at Banchory, at first under the supervision of David Dean, a local man who was appointed locomotive foreman in 1854. Unfortunately he had to be dismissed six years later for misappropriation of funds and departed to New Zealand. His place was taken by his brother Hugh, the shop foreman, who must have satisfied the management as in 1864 they increased his salary

This coach was built as a 1st class for the Deeside Railway and survived for use on excursion trains until 1924. Luxurious to start with, but doubtless spartan at the end! It had been downgraded to a 1st/3rd composite by the GNS when this photo was taken.

The old Deeside Railway Works still stand as a reminder of busier days at Banchory, the Deeside terminus from 1853 to 1859.

from £110 to £115 plus a free house, fuel and light. After the Deeside amalgamated with the Great North the writing was on the wall for the Banchory Works. Mr Dean was paid off and left the Company at the end of March 1879 with two months salary as a reward for 23 years service.

Under the terms of the lease it was a condition that all the Deeside stock retained their own numbers. This proved too much for the Great North's locomotive superintendent, William Cowan, who found himself with another eight engines having the same numbers as eight of his own, so he did the sensible thing and re-numbered them, never mind what the lease said.

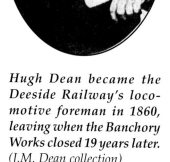

All the Hawthorns had been withdrawn by 1883 and for the next 50 years Great North engines, mostly moderate sized 4-4-0s, reigned virtually supreme apart from the suburban services to Culter. For most of their existence these were handled by the 0-4-4 tank engines built for this purpose, although they also worked to Ballater on occasions.

Hugh Dean became the Deeside Railway's locomotive foreman in 1860, leaving when the Banchory Works closed 19 years later. (J.M. Dean collection)

When the LNER assumed ownership at first little changed. Then in the mid 1920s some ex-North British Railway engines of Class D31, also 4-4-0s, were transferred to Aberdeen and no doubt they took their place on Deeside workings. An interesting arrival in 1929 was Sentinel steam railcar *Highland Chieftain*, one of a series built in an attempt to reduce costs. It ran for a period of about 12 months principally on suburban trains out to Dyce and Culter with some duties taking it as far as Banchory. Two years later saw the

Down Deeside express on Dinnet Moor in 1908; Class T engine No.101.

A former Great Eastern Railway Class B12 No.61532 approaches Ferryhill Junction from Deeside. These engines first appeared in the north-east in 1931, although this one did not arrive until June 1946. It was withdrawn from service thirteen years later. (John Robertson, B.P. Hoper Collection)

One of the BR standard 2-6-4 tank engines has just crossed Beltie Viaduct with a Ballater train on the climb to Satan's Den.

appearance of real strangers when former Great Eastern Railway 4-6-0s of Class B12 came north. These natives of East Anglia were much larger than anything yet seen in the North-east and to start with were prohibited from working beyond Banchory. The final year before the LNER was absorbed into British Railways brought the Class B1 4-6-0s, these being the first brand new engines on Great North metals for over 25 years.

As in 1923, so in 1948 when the Deeside line became part of British Railways, the status quo continued for the first few years. The early 1950s saw the new standard 2-6-4 tank engines begin to take over much of the work, but because the locomotives working the line were supplied by Kittybrewster depot in Aberdeen, members of other classes were not infrequently rostered, but it would be tedious to try and mention them all.

Until 1958 all the trains were steam hauled. April of that year saw the arrival of the unique electric rail-car, which deserves special note. Essentially it was a standard diesel multiple-unit with the engines replaced by electric motors supplied from large batteries housed underneath the floors. These were re-charged at both ends of the journey although it is said that the drivers never really trusted the Aberdeen staff to do the job properly and were glad to reach Ballater safely! It was a wonderful experience travelling in it as it was almost silent. Generally speaking it performed well but by 1962 problems were arising and it was withdrawn but not scrapped. Instead it spent several years with the BR Research Unit until it was put up for disposal in 1984. Even that was not the end. It has now been returned to it's former territory and can be seen at the Royal Deeside Railway Preservation Society's base at Milton of Crathes. From June 1958 until all passenger services were withdrawn, the ubiquitous diesel multiple-units worked those turns not covered by the battery car while, during 1960, diesel-electric locomotives, usually English Electric Type

The battery rail-car passes Aboyne Loch on a May evening in 1960. (The late Roy Hamilton)

A Ballater-bound DMU passes Tullich Lodge, just outside Ballater, with the Culblean Hills in the background.

1 (Class 20) and North British Locomotive Co's Type 2 (Class 21), began to handle the freight trains.

Finally there were the shunting engines, known as 'pugs', owned by the Culter paper mill. When the rail system there was enlarged around the turn of the century it was apparently first worked by a small electric locomotive although no details seem to have survived. It was scrapped around 1920 when the Company bought a standard 0-4-0 tank engine from Messrs Peckett of Bristol. This lasted until 1954 when it was replaced by a similar engine built by the same makers and acquired second hand. Both looked very smart in their green livery with red frames and buffer beams and carrying a large brass plate on the cab side showing the builder's name.

One of the North British Locomotive Company's Type 2 diesel-electrics (subsequently Class 21) approaches Cults with a down goods train in 1966. The poor reliability of this class made them hated by the men of Inverurie Works who had to maintain them.

Over the years, several classes of engine came north to work on the former GNSR lines. Here No.40603, ex-LMSR, passes the site of Ruthrieston Station with a train of ex-LNER Gresleys for Ballater. (Colonel A.D. McKenzie. Courtesy Mr K. Dallas)

The Culter Paper Mill's second 'pug' was built by Messrs Peckett of Bristol in 1941, coming north in 1954.

Culter Mills. The wire-strung poles on the left may have been for an electric loco. (Aberdeen University Library, G.W. Wilson Collection)

Forest, farm and paper

Deeside is essentially rural in character with many farms and forests, the upper reaches in particular being well wooded, and over the years timber provided much of the outward traffic generated above Banchory. The old road and even the turnpike did not solve the problem of getting it to its main market in Aberdeen. The solution lay in floating the logs down the river which was all very well provided it was properly controlled. If it was not, there could be trouble. The bridge at Potarch, a couple of miles below Kincardine O'Neill, was badly damaged during construction in 1812 due to careless floating and this led directly to an Act of Parliament regulating the operation in Scotland which was not repealed for over 150 years — long after the demise of floating.

The value of this trade was apparent to the promoters of the Deeside Railway who estimated an income of around £2,000 per year from this source alone and it was not long before the line benefited from the traffic. Within a couple of months of opening a contractor was appointed to load timber at Banchory. The "floating bank" on the river at Crathes closed in the late 1850s while a siding laid in to serve the sawmill at Silverstripe, about $^1/_2$ mile east of Banchory, remained in use for over 100 years.

Further up the valley the directors of the Aboyne and Braemar had anticipated carrying 12-14,000 tons per year but were sadly disappointed when during 1868 only some 3,500 tons reached Ballater from Ballochbuie and other forests on Upper Deeside. This was largely due to traction engines being unable to cope with the dreadful roads, hence the need for a tramway to Bridge of Gairn, but before this could be built, Ballochbuie was sold to Queen Victoria who did not exploit its trees.

The importance of this source of income remained over the years, at least until after the last war. It is reasonable to assume, for example, that much of the 3000 tons of goods dispatched from the small wayside station at Dinnet during 1938 arose from timber.

During both world wars demand rose to new heights and this put a great deal of pressure on the Deeside line and its staff. In 1943 over 100 wagons could be loaded and dispatched daily from the various stations although much of it was concentrated at Ballater where two new sidings were provided especially for this purpose. In all, over half a million tons were sent out during the period 1939-45, much of it provided by the Canadian 'lumber-jacks' who had set up three camps in the valley.

Agriculture provided its share of business with feed stuffs and live stock being notable in this respect. Again taking the 1938 figures, Aboyne and Ballater between them handled nearly 11,000 head of livestock although this particular source of income had less impact further down the line. After declining over the years it finally came to an end in BR days.

Especially in the years before the 1914-18 war, general merchandise figured large, with coal being an important import; although this again declined over the years with the ever increasing use of other forms of fuel.

Paper may seem a strange commodity when considering this essentially rural railway but the mill at Culter played an important part in the line's economics. It was first made in the vicinity about 1696, then in 1751, Bartholomew Smith converted the old Waulkmill of Craigton into a paper mill making use of the water from the Culter Burn running alongside.

A siding to serve this mill had been provided by the early 1860s but, by the turn of the century, traffic had grown to the extent that further sidings had been laid down leading into the mill itself. Not only did the raw materials required arrive by rail but also the very large amounts of coal needed. Even as late as the mid-1950s some 600 tons were received each week. Add the fact that most of the mill's output also went by rail and it will be seen that all in all it generated a good deal of traffic. Although inward and outward movements continued up to the end, amounts fell off for various reasons, including of course the rising popularity of road haulage especially on the short haul to and from Aberdeen docks, but the serious railway strike of 1955 undoubtedly played a large part in this.

Signalling

The Deeside Railway being single track the company had to provide a certificate to the effect that only one engine, or two coupled together, would at any one time be allowed between any two stations — an undertaking which had to be included in the Company's Rule Book. Train movements were controlled by telegraph communication between the stations, a simple system which relied for its safety on strict discipline which was seldom lacking. So there never was a "cornfield meet", as the Americans called it.

This method of working continued until the Regulation of Railways Act, 1889, came into force which required that not only had signals and points to be interlocked so that they worked in conjunction with each other, but each driver on a single line had to be in possession of a token giving his train the sole right to occupy the line between signal boxes. On most railways the tokens were exchanged between the signalman and the engine crew by hand, with obvious dangers to both when done on the move. In the late 1880s James Manson, the Great North's locomotive superintendent, developed an apparatus by which this could be done safely by non-stopping trains and this was brought into use on Deeside during the early months of 1895.

When the line opened to Banchory there were no passing loops and even when it reached Ballater trains could still only cross at Banchory. Clearly this limited the number that could be worked although there was provision to cross them by the simple, but time consuming, expedient of shunting one into a siding. Over the years crossing loops were added until finally only Glassel, Dess and Cambus O'May lacked them.

Increasing traffic, especially in the suburban area, led to the provision of double track between Ferryhill and Park, the work being done in stages, reaching West Cults in July 1884, Culter eight years later and Park in 1899. Although the original intention was to have double track as far as Banchory, this was never carried out. The whole length reverted to single track on 2nd December 1951 with Culter and Park becoming passing loops. The habits of years apparently died hard as the first down train the following day left Culter on the newly closed track where it collided with a temporary buffer stop, the engine and leading bogie of the first vehicle being derailed but fortunately without injury to anybody.

With the general run-down in traffic the various signal boxes were closed over the years. Drum was the first to go in 1950 followed by Cults in 1953 and Crathes the following year. The withdrawal of the passenger service in February 1966 saw Torphins, Lumphanan and Dinnet closed completely, goods traffic having already ceased, with the remainder reduced to the status of ground frames controlling the station sidings. The goods trains thereafter worked on the system known as "one engine in steam" — even though by this time steam engines had disappeared(!) — the driver being given a token at Ferryhill which covered the whole line.

Snow clearing near Murtle at the end of December 1908.

Snow

Although snow was a regular winter feature along Deeside, and indeed had an unfortunate effect soon after the opening to Ballater, it did not normally lead to any great hindrance to running the trains. Occasionally, however, matters were very different.

The earliest account relates to a severe storm during the last week of December 1878. On Saturday 21st, which was "rather wild", trains ran more or less normally until the last down service from Aberdeen, which left Aboyne about half an hour late. During a further lengthy delay at Dinnet the passengers, by now feeling rather exasperated and no doubt very cold, as trains had no heating in those days, were told that the engine had gone ahead to clear the line. Eventually it returned and the train headed out over the Muir of Dinnet but had not gone far before it came to a stand as once again the engine set off to clear the line. While this was going on the guard moved all the passengers into the front carriage with the intention of leaving the rest where they were and hoping to get through with a lighter load. Still no sign of the engine; which had indeed become snowed up within a few yards of the train. Eventually a dozen or so passengers "including three young ladies" set off on foot for Cambus O'May. To begin with it was a light-hearted party but by the time they reached the station the "weaker vessels" were glad to spend the night in the surfaceman's cottage. The men carried on but three had given up by the time they reached Tullich while the rest struggled on to Ballater. Next day a rescue party set out and brought the ladies and mail bags home on a sleigh.

The last serious blockage was in January 1960. Monday 18th saw heavy falls of snow which later eased off but by Tuesday evening blizzard conditions prevailed only to be followed by glorious sunshine the next day. There was widespread dislocation throughout northern Scotland, the Deeside line being no exception. Conditions were so bad that the normal rail-cars could not operate and steam trains took their place. Even so, they only managed to reach Banchory on Thursday, although by that evening they did get through to Torphins. An engine with a normal snowplough then managed to reach Lumphanan before having to retreat. Next the drifts were attacked by a larger engine with a big snowplough accompanied by two coaches of workmen equipped with shovels. Eventually they were able to force a way through allowing the evening train on Friday 22nd to reach Ballater. Meantime those scholars from Torphins attending Banchory Academy were marooned there for a couple of days until eventually getting home in the back of a Land Rover.

The staff of Aberdeen (Deeside) Goods Station in 1877. Mr Fowler, the Agent, is seen on the right of the front row.

The first bus on the service from Ballater, an 18 seat Milnes-Daimler registration number SA 74, seen at Braemar on 2nd May 1904. The conductor is on the left, while the driver (centre) carries an oil-can. On the right are the local policeman and the GNSR 'stationmaster'. The building still survives. (Keith Jones collection)

Bus services

At first sight it may seem strange to include buses in a book about the Deeside Line but the Great North of Scotland was one of the earliest railway companies to recognise their value as feeders to the trains, only the Great Western and North Eastern Railways in England preceding it by some 12 months.

The honour of being their first route fell to that between Ballater and Braemar which began running on 2nd May 1904 with two return services on weekdays connecting in and out of the trains, and allowed about 1hr 30 mins for the 17 mile journey at a single fare of 2/6. Three years later the Company secured the contract for running the mails to Braemar which involved an extra bus on Sunday. This meant that apart from the Messenger trains, it was the only GNSR vehicle in public service on the Sabbath.

To begin with the Company had no legal authority to run buses and before long the highway authorities started to claim for damage alleged to have been done by them. It was not until 1906 the situation was regularised.

Bad weather or heavy snow could cause severe problems and to reduce delay to trains at Ballater the buses left Braemar 15 minutes earlier in these conditions, which must have caused problems to the unwary. If the bus could not get through for any reason the conductor had the additional problem of carrying the mail bag to its destination regardless of the weather! In the days before breakdown vehicles, horses had to come to the rescue of any bus in trouble, no doubt bringing many a smile on the faces of the old coachmen.

The route remained railway owned until 1930 when it was transferred to Messrs Alexander but as the LNER was a shareholder in that firm it continued to benefit, if in a minor way, from the ticket moneys. To-day (2008) the service is operated by Bluebird, part of the Stagecoach group, with the original bus depot behind the Invercauld Arms still surviving.

For a short time there was another route based on the line. June 1905 saw the introduction of a bus between Culter station and Midmar, about 12 miles to the north-west, but clearly this did not pay as it was withdrawn some 18 months later and replaced by a new service running direct from Aberdeen, thus avoiding the inconvenience of a change of vehicle on such a short journey.

Two GNSR buses at Bellabeg, Strathdon. The one on the right has come from Ballater while SA 172 on the left has probably arrived from Alford. Both were made by Milnes-Daimler.

Unfulfilled dreams

As was so often the case elsewhere, there were proposals for other railways affecting the Deeside line.

In the 1850s considerable interest was shown in the idea of a railway to Alford, a market town in Strathdon some 18 miles north-west of Culter. Various proposals were made for a branch from the main GNSR line and while these were being considered the Deeside Railway produced its own plans in 1855 for reaching Alford. The first of these involved extending from Banchory to Lumphanan and continuing via Cushnie. A possible route was surveyed but the scheme was dropped in favour of a branch from near Drum which would have run via Echt and Tillyfourie. A new company, The Deeside and Alford Valley Extension Railway, was promoted and a public meeting in Alford overwhelmingly supported this against the rival scheme leaving the GNSR at Kintore. Parliament, however, did not approve and the Deeside's proposal was dropped.

In the early 1880s an extraordinary proposal appeared which arose out of the antagonism existing between the Great North and Highland companies. Because the latter made life difficult when it came to exchanging traffic to and from Inverness at Keith and Elgin, the Great North sought ways of mitigating the situation with a new route connecting its Speyside branch with Inverness, thus avoiding the problems. This would have meant their trains using the twisty, and therefore slow, line up the Spey from Craigellachie. However at the same time a group of north-east lairds put forward their own proposal for the Strathspey, Strathdon and Deeside Junction Railway connecting Cambus O'May with the Speyside line at Nethybridge. The intervening country was virtually uninhabited but they justified the 40 mile route with its steep gradients and four tunnels on the basis that it would serve granite quarries and iron ore deposits known to exist in the area. Combined, these two proposals apparently provided the Great North with an alternative route between Aberdeen and Inverness but neither received Parliamentary approval. Many years later internal correspondence revealed that the Company's chairman and general manager had an even more grandiose scheme in mind involving a completely new railway from Dundee to Ballater, which, making use of these other proposed lines, would have created a direct route from Dundee to Inverness.

Perhaps the strangest unfulfilled dream concerns what happened to the Aboyne and Braemar Railway which never went beyond Ballater, some 16 miles short of its intended destination. If it had been built it would have more or less followed the line of the present main road, crossing the Dee a mile or so below the Old Bridge of Invercauld and ending in Braemar with a station on the comparatively level ground near the Invercauld Arms Hotel. Even before this proposal was embodied in the company's Act of Parliament the section beyond Ballater had disappeared to be replaced by a tramway $1\frac{1}{2}$ miles long to Bridge of Gairn and restricted to goods traffic only. This would have connected

The proposed railway to Braemar finally petered out in a field at Bridge of Gairn, a mere mile and a half beyond Ballater.

with a further tramway which Colonel Farquharson of Invercauld proposed to make serving his forest at Ballochbuie, but before any work was done Queen Victoria leased (and later bought) Ballochbuie, commercial exploitation ceased and with it the need for the tramway.

That, at least, was the official position and as late as 1921 was repeated by the GNSR's lawyer in a memorandum. By contrast, right from the start the local people were firmly of the opinion that the Queen herself had vetoed the proposal for the line to reach Braemar so as to retain her privacy at Balmoral. When the Deeside Railway Company's minute books became available they were found to contain a letter from Mr A.W.White, the Queen's Private Solicitor, showing that this was indeed the case.

In the end all that was built was the short length to Bridge of Gairn, hence the overbridge just beyond Ballater station. The trackbed now forms a pleasant walk through the woods above the Dee while the abutments of the bridge built to take the rails over the River Gairn carry a water supply pipe.

In 1897 the directors investigated the possibility of a hotel at Bridge of Gairn to be served by extending the track from Ballater. They decided to seek the Queen's approval but early in the following year it was clear that this would not be forthcoming and the proposal was abandoned.

Even that was not the end of the story. The company intended to start a bus service between Ballater and Braemar in 1904 and late the previous year looked into the possibility of using the track formation as a reserved right-of-way out as far as the Gairn. It seems the cost would have been too great and the idea was dropped.

The end of the line

Dr Beeching is generally regarded as the author of the proposal to close the Deeside line but in fact this was first considered by British Railways as early as November 1950. Although no further action was taken at the time it was included among the many lines to be closed under the Beeching Report published in 1963. Originally the passenger service was to be withdrawn on 2nd March 1964 but this was bitterly opposed with a local committee being set up for this purpose. An appeal to the Transport Users Consultative Committee was rejected and on 31st August 1965 the Minister of Transport decreed that no real hardship would arise from the loss of rail services. Following that, British Railways announced that passenger trains would cease to run as from 28th February 1966.

The last passenger train was the 8.35pm from Aberdeen on

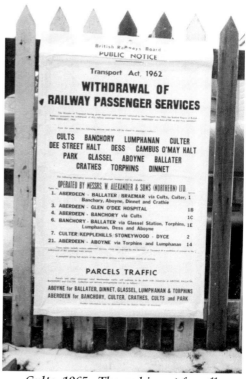

Cults, 1965. The end is not far off.

Saturday 26th February and quite a number of people made use of the fact that it had to return to Aberdeen as empty stock to make a final, unofficial, round trip. A large crowd awaited the train's arrival at Ballater and the hostelry on the station did a roaring trade — indeed it was reported that certain liquids had run dry! Mr W.Stewart, the stationmaster, summoned the passengers with the century old handbell and the train left to a broadside of detonators. All along the line the lights went out for the last time and an otherwise merry occasion was tinged with sadness at the redundancy of so many railwaymen. This final train arrived at Platform 6 in the Joint Station at 11.38pm where two ticket collectors awaited it and led the passengers in single file out of the station.

Thus it was that after just over 100 years passengers were no longer able to enjoy this very scenic journey. If the trains had survived just a few more years modern signalling systems could have greatly reduced running costs and, who knows, perhaps we would still have been able to see the beautiful scenery from the comfort of a railway carriage.

Goods trains to Ballater lingered on for a further 5 months after which they were cut back to Culter, due largely to the presence of the paper mill in that town. Even then the end was not far off and the very last train on Deeside ran on 30th December 1966. For once a sad occasion was graced with sunshine and in honour of the event the usual diesel was replaced by Class B1 No.61180 from Dundee which looked surprisingly clean as its black livery gleamed in the winter sun. The outward train left Guild Street at 10.40am and consisted of four goods brake vans carrying some thirty people who had all bought a return First Class ticket costing 6/6 ($32\frac{1}{2}$p) for the privilege! The driver, Frank Duncan, had driven Deeside trains, including the Royal train for the past 23 years and was glad to have a steam engine for the occasion but the fireman, who had not handled a shovel for five years said his hands were feeling it! The guard, Bob Taylor, was another Deeside man.

It seems appropriate considering the line's association with timber haulage that the final seven wagons lifted at Culter should contain timber destined for the railway works at Inverurie and Derby. The train set off on its return journey leaving John Robb to close the station and become the last railwayman to serve on the Deeside Line. At Ferryhill Junction the single line tablet was handed back to the signalman for the last time. The points were locked over for ever and 113 years, 3 months and 22 days of history came to an end.

Or had it? In recent years the Royal Deeside Railway Preservation Society has put in a good deal of work with the aim of re-opening at least part of the route and trains once again roll along a short section of the line.

The very last train on Deeside. Class B1 No.61180 is well polished up for the occasion as it arrives at Culter on 30th December 1966.

What is left?

Although the railway closed during 1966 track lifting did not start until 6th April 1970. Some years later Aberdeen District Council created the Deeside Walkway between Duthie Park and Culter, a pleasant stroll and well worth a visit. Other lengths now attractive walks are from Crathes to Banchory and again from Dinnet to Ballater and on through the woods below Craigendarroch to Bridge of Gairn, using the track of the abortive extension to Braemar.

In the suburban area only the buildings at Pitfodels, Murtle and Cults remain. The latter is used as a workshop, the other two being private houses. Further station buildings converted to houses are Crathes, where the signal box has been re-built, Glassel, Dess and Cambus O'May. Park is used by a caravan dealer, while Dinnet houses the local estate office.

The Royal Deeside Railway Preservation Society are now based at Milton of Crathes, opposite the entrance to Crathes Castle. Here it has built a new station and established a collection of rolling stock, including the Battery Railcar which has returned to Deeside. Tracklaying is proceeding towards the outskirts of Banchory and by summer 2007 brake van rides were available to the public.

The station building at Aboyne, now surrounded by tarmac, is owned by Aberdeenshire Council who let it out as shops and offices, while the tunnel is now a small-bore rifle range. Ballater, also owned by the Council, is a Category B Listed Building in recognition of its historic importance. It has been fully restored and is in use as a visitor centre, with tourist office, restaurant and exhibition which includes memorabilia, tableaux and a replica royal carriage of 1869. This was formally unveiled by the Duke and Duchess of Rothesay in April 2008.

At Banchory, Torphins and Lumphanan it is difficult to realise that the railway ever existed. All that remains at Banchory are the old Deeside Company's engine shed, now used as workshops, and one or two other small buildings, with the massive retaining wall built by the Great North to protect its property from the river still performing the same function. Most of the

This ex-army engine built by Hunslet in 1940 is seen here 30 years later in contractor's service during demolition work at Banchory.

old railway yard is now covered by houses. At Torphins and Lumphanan again the sites are occupied by houses but interestingly at Torphins the road layout has reverted to what it was before the railway came. The road from Kincardine O'Neill to Inverurie once more has a clear run north from the square although the diversionary road and bridge provided when the station was built are still in use.

For much of the way the track bed can still be seen but inevitably nature and man have, over the years, had their effect. Indeed imagination is needed to picture the Deeside line as an active, working railway, but is well worth the effort.

Bibliography

Aboyne and Braemar Railway Minute Books

Deeside Railway Minute Books and Papers

Great North of Scotland Railway Minute Books

LNER Papers

Board of Trade Inspection Reports

Aberdeen Directory, 1824 - 25 and 1850 - 51

Great North Review (various issues)

The Great North of Scotland Railway — A Guide   W. Ferguson of Kinmundy
David Douglas (1881)

The Great North of Scotland Railway   Sir M. Barclay-Harvey
Locomotive Publishing Co. (1940)

The Great North of Scotland Railway (2nd Edition)   H.A. Vallance
David St.John Thomas (1989)

Regional History of the Railways of Great Britain Vol. 15   J. Thomas & D. Turnock
David St.John Thomas (1989)

Industrial Locomotives of Scotland
Industrial Railway Society (1976)

The Old Deeside Road   G.M. Fraser
Aberdeen Natural History & Antiquarian Society (1921)
Robin Callander (1980/81/82/83)

The "Subbies"   K.G. Jones
G.N.S.R.A. (1987)

The Royal Deeside Line   A.D. Farr
David and Charles (1968)

Stories and Tales of Royal Deeside's Railway   A.D. Farr
Kestrel Books (1971)

Opening and closing dates

Station	Miles [1]	Opened		Closed	
		Passenger	Goods	Passenger	Goods
Ferryhill Junction	0 5/8	8:9:1853	8:9:1853	2:8:1854	2:8:1854
Holburn Street	1 3/8	2:7:1894	—	5:4:1937	—
Ruthrieston	1 3/4	1854 (1856?)	—	5:4:1937	—
Pitfodels	3	2:7:1894	—	5:4:1937	—
Cults	3 5/8	8:9:1853	8:9:1853	28:2:1966	15:6:1964
West Cults	4 1/4	1:8:1894	—	5:4:1937	—
Bieldside	4 3/4	1:6:1897	—	5:4:1937	—
Murtle	5 3/8	8:9:1853	8:9:1853	5:4:1937	5:4:1937
Milltimber	6 1/4	1854	1854(?)	5:4:1937	5:4:1937
Culter	7 3/8	8:9:1853	8:9:1853	28:2:1966	2:1:1967
Drum	9 3/4	1854	1854(?)	10:9:1951	10:9:1951
Park	10 3/4	8:9:1853	8:9:1853	28:2:1966	15:6:1964
Mills of Drum	12 7/8	8:9:1853	—	1:1:1863	—
Crathes	14 1/4	1:1:1863	1:1:1863	28:2:1966	15:6:1964
Crathes Castle [2]	14 1/4	8:9:1853	—	1:1:1863	—
Banchory	16 3/4	8:9:1853	8:9:1853	28:2:1966	18:7:1966
Dee Street	17 1/2	6:2:1961	—	28:2:1966	—
Glassel [3]	21 3/8	2:12:1859	2:12:1859	28:2:1966	15:6:1964
Torphins	23 3/4	2:12:1859	2:12:1859	28:2:1966	29:3:1965
Lumphanan	26 7/8	2:12:1859	2:12:1859	28:2:1966	15:6:1964
Dess	29 1/2	2:12:1859	2:12:1859	28:2:1966	1:7:1960
Aboyne [4]	32 1/4	2:12:1859	2:12:1859	28:2:1966	18:7:1966
Dinnet	36 3/4	17:10:1866	17:10:1866	28:2:1966	15:6:1964
Cambus O'May	39 3/8	4:10:1875	4:10:1875	28:2:1966	?
Ballater	43 1/4	17:10:1866	17:10:1866	28:2:1966	18:7:1966

Opening and closing dates: notes

1. The distances are as given in working documents and shown on the mileposts which were measured from zero in the Joint Station. As neither the GNSR nor the LNER owned the first $^5/_8$ mile out to Ferryhill Junction they make the branch appear to be that much longer than it really was.

2. Crathes Castle was a private station.

3. For a few years prior to 1887 there was a private platform for the owner of Craigmyle House between Glassel and Torphins.

4. At various times between 1888 and 1939 a temporary platform was in use at Aboyne Loch, about a mile east of the station, for excursions in the summer and bonspiels in the winter.

Provision of double track

Ferryhill Junction to Cults	14th June	1884
Cults to Murtle	13th July	1892
Murtle to Culter	24th Sept	1892
Culter to Park	28th Aug	1899

Track singled

2nd Dec 1951

Occasionally the timetable showed simultaneous departures from Aberdeen of trains to Ballater and the south. On 12th August 1955, a beautifully clean No.80110 (left) sets out with the 6.05pm for Deeside while an ex-LMSR Class 5 is in charge of the train to Stonehaven. The ex-Caley 0-6-0T also appears to be joining in the race! (The late E.N.C. Haywood)

Cults — 1901

Culter — 1865

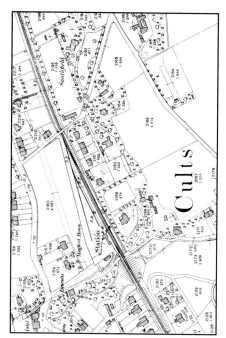

Lying close to Aberdeen, it is clear that goods traffic had only a small part to play in the life of the station.

The maps of selected stations on the Deeside line are taken from the Ordnance Survey 25" to 1 mile series.

They have been reduced by 50% for reproduction here. Towards Aberdeen is at the top of the page.

Grey areas are not covered by the map sheet.

0 *yards*   100   200   300

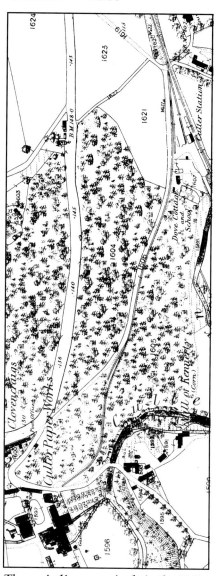

The main line was single in the 1860s, and one siding sufficed for the paper mill traffic.

Abbreviations: FB - Footbridge; GP - Guide Post; MP - Mile Post; PO - Post Office;

Culter Mill — 1899

Culter Station — 1899

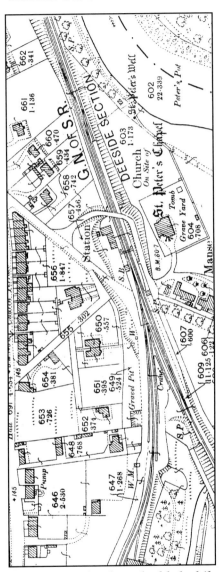

Culter Mill has now greatly expanded and includes a network of sidings.

The main line has been doubled while the station has been rebuilt some distance east.

SB - Signal Box; SP - Signal Post; WM - Weighing Machine

Banchory — 1864

Banchory — 1925

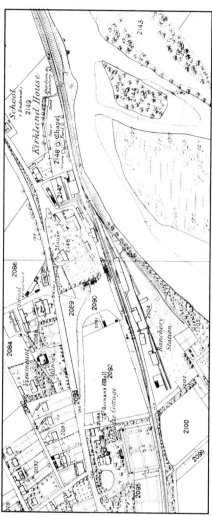

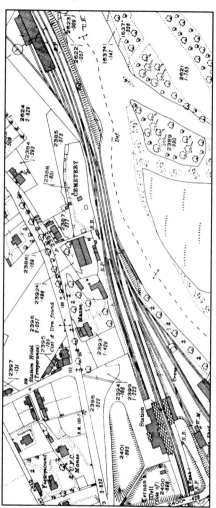

The original station was a simple affair with the locomotive works at the eastern end.

The station has been rebuilt further west and the whole layout greatly enlarged. The works are completely isolated and replaced by the new engine sheds to the east.

Abbreviations: FB - Footbridge;   FP - Footpath;   P - Pump;
PO - Post Office;   SB - Signal Box;   SP - Signal Post;   WM - Weighing Machine

Torphins — 1899

Aboyne — 1899

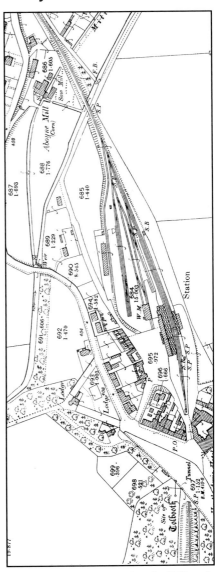

Before the railway, Station Road continued straight on but was replaced by Bridge Street. Now it is once again a through road.

To-day the main station building is all that remains of this once extensive layout.

Ballater — 1866

Ballater — 1923

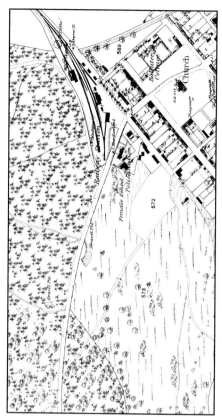

The original station was a small and simple layout when compared with what was to come.

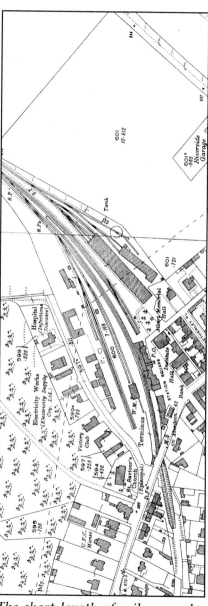

Abbrev: C - Crane; MP - Mile Post;
MS - Mile Stone; PO - Post Office;
SB - Signal Box; SP - Signal Post;
WM - Weighing Machine

The short length of railway under the bridge was to be the start of the ex-tension to Braemar.

1864 Passenger traffic
(12 months to 31ˢᵗ August, 1864)

Deeside Railway

	Forwarded	Received	Total
Aberdeen	128,170 $^1/_2$	94,912	223,082 $^1/_2$
Ruthrieston	483	473	956
Cults	19,855	32,744	52,599
Murtle	6,053 $^1/_2$	6,418	12,471 $^1/_2$
Milltimber	4,764 $^1/_2$	2,339	7,103 $^1/_2$
Culter	17,863	20,617 $^1/_2$	38,480 $^1/_2$
Drum	6,656 $^1/_2$	6,502	13,158 $^1/_2$
Park	12,703	13,534	26,237
Crathes	9,642	6,447 $^1/_2$	16,089 $^1/_2$
Banchory	22,086 $^1/_2$	39,900	61,996 $^1/_2$

Deeside Extension Railway

	Forwarded	Received	Total
Banchory	4,286 $^1/_2$	5,058	9,344 $^1/_2$
Glassel	4,296	3,529 $^1/_2$	7,825 $^1/_2$
Torphins	8,629 $^1/_2$	8,237	16,886 $^1/_2$
Lumphanan	8 967 $^1/_2$	6,984 $^1/_2$	15,952
Dess	3,642 $^1/_2$	2,765	6,407 $^1/_2$
Aboyne	14,656 $^1/_2$	22,295 $^1/_2$	36,952

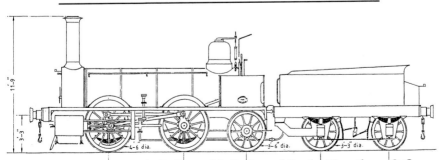

Deeside Railway No.5. One of five by Hawthorn & Co, Leith. Built in 1859, withdrawn 1876. (Hugh Gordon)

1864 Goods and Livestock traffic
(12 months to 31ˢᵗ August, 1864)

Deeside Railway

	Goods (tons)			Livestock (head)		
	Forwarded	*Received*	*Total*	*Forwarded*	*Received*	*Total*
Aberdeen	28,758	23,285	52,043	194	3,730	3,924
Cults	39	2,917	2,956	—	30	30
Murtle	58	809	867	11	4	15
Milltimber	95	136	231	—	—	—
Culter	5,708	7,294	13,002	4	4	8
Drum	277	652	929	77	8	85
Park	1,578	1,849	3,427	119	14	133
Crathes	1,780	1,099	2,879	109	9	118
Banchory	4,902	7,105	12,007	1,533	57	1,590

Deeside Extension Railway

	Goods (tons)			Livestock (head)		
	Forwarded	*Received*	*Total*	*Forwarded*	*Received*	*Total*
Banchory	98	130	228	—	54	54
Glassel	106	170	276	160	1	161
Torphins	1,658	1,316	2,974	183	7	190
Lumphanan	2,639	1,296	3,935	398	13	411
Dess	421	266	687	21	11	32
Aboyne	5,273	5,076	10,349	1,199	66	1,265

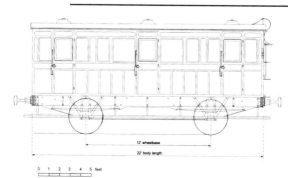

Deeside Railway, 1st Class, Nos. 1-5. Brown & Marshall supplied these 28 seaters in 1854-55. One survived long enough to be allocated a number by the LNER. (Keith Fenwick)

1938 Traffic

Passengers

	Tickets	£
Cults	3,669	393
Culter	6,572	375
Drum	378	17
Park	836	119
Crathes	1,058	105
Banchory	13,390	1,423
Glassel	1,262	121
Torphins	6,666	718
Lumphanan	3,233	289
Dess	681	52
Aboyne	6,552	1,557
Dinnet	1,926	325
Ballater	8,194	2,165

Goods and Livestock

	Received (tons)			Forw'd'd (tons)	Livestock (head)	
	General	Coal	Total	General	Rec'v'd	Forw'd'd
Cults	924	185	1,109	20		
Culter	25,115	22,106	47,221	9,277		
Drum*	—	—	—	—		
Park	142	61	203	545		
Crathes*	—	—	—	—		
Banchory	1,494	2,278	3,772	9,309		
Glassel (included in Torphins)						
Torphins	475	827	1,302	1,979		
Lumphanan	1,522	77	1,599	267		
Dess (included in Aboyne)						
Aboyne	4,033	2,323	6,356	5,057	2,824	6,500
Dinnet	467	134	601	3,031		
Ballater	2,008	3,266	5,274	1,791	2,449	—

*No records for Crathes or Drum (included in Banchory and Culter respectively?)

Livestock

Other stations — only minimal

Acknowledgements

Grateful thanks are due to those who assisted with this booklet, in particular fellow members of the GNSR Association, including George Boardman, Keith Fenwick, Keith Jones, the late Ed Nicol, Martin Smith and Mike Stephen.

All photographs are drawn from the Association's archives except where shown.

As always, the Librarian and Staff at the National Archives of Scotland (formerly the Scottish Record Office) and the Map Section of the National Library of Scotland have been cheerfully helpful.

The 25" OS maps are reproduced by kind permission of the Trustees of the National Library of Scotland.

Editorial —   Dick Jackson

Layout & typesetting —   George Boardman

First Published by the Great North of Scotland Railway Association 1999.
Revised and reprinted 2001 and 2008. © 2008 GNSRA. All rights reserved.

Amend ISBN 978 0 90234309 2

Printed by XIC www.xic.com

design
marketing
print

About this book:

In 1994, the Association published 'The Deeside Line', now out of print.

'Royal Deeside's Railway' is a new book, containing entirely different photographs and illustrations from those used in 'The Deeside Line', plus OS maps and new text which includes much additional information, as well as full colour.

The Great North of Scotland Railway Association

The Association was formed in 1964 to cater for all those interested in recording the history of the former Great North of Scotland Railway and its constituent companies.

Membership:

Membership is open to anybody interested in furthering the aims of the Association. Details may be obtained by visiting our website www.gnsra.org.uk